To St. Mark's Library
and its faithful public
James C. Fahey —

General Redemptorist Army
Nov. 19, 1981

Ministry and Solitude

MINISTRY AND SOLITUDE

The Ministry of the Laity
and the Clergy
in Church and Society

James C. Fenhagen

THE SEABURY PRESS : NEW YORK

1981
The Seabury Press
815 Second Avenue
New York, N.Y. 10017

Printed in the United States of America

Library of Congress Cataloging in Publication Data

Fenhagen, James C.
Ministry and solitude.
Includes bibliographical references.
1. Pastoral theology. I. Title.
BV4011.F43   253   81-14398
ISBN 0-8164-0498-4

AACR2

In memoriam
Urban T. Holmes, III

Contents

Introduction

During the early days of my ministry I had the good fortune to meet one of the most remarkable women I've ever known. By the time we met she was already rather old and quite fearless—indeed, at times even fearsome. Her sharp tongue was devastating, particularly when she was faced with hypocrisy or mindless sentimentality. Beneath this sharp exterior, however, was a woman with a large heart and a social conscience to match.

I met my elderly friend after preaching my first sermon in a church I was to serve for a number of years. In the time allotted for congregational response to what I had said, she took me on. I don't remember what she said. I only remember that I was devastated by the sharpness and unexpectedness of her remarks. As time went on, however, I got to know her better, and the more I came to know her, the greater were my respect and affection.

Some time later my friend became seriously ill and was taken to the hospital. I went to see her, not knowing whether she would ever leave that hospital alive. As I stood outside her door, preparing to go in, I felt fearful that what I would say to her would evoke what I had experienced before. As I entered the room my anxiety continued to grow; and as I often do when I am anxious, I began to talk. I don't know how long this went on—probably only a few minutes. I only know that what I said seemed painfully disconnected from what I was really feeling. As I stood there, talking away, she slowly reached up and took my hand. "Jim," she said, in words similar to these, "I want to share with you something it has taken me a lifetime to learn: In the silence, Christ can heal."

I have never forgotten that experience, or the remarkable Christian who taught me so much. Her life reflected what she believed. Although fiercely independent, she was rooted in the worshipping community of which she was so integral a part. Her passion for justice and peace had been nurtured in those deep places within her where she and the Lord Jesus Christ had come to speak on intimate terms. From my friend I came to learn that ministry and solitude were not separate at all, but one and the same thing; without one, the other could not exist.

This book is about what I saw incarnated in my friend. It is written for the Christian clergy and laity who are concerned about ways of more fully sharing in Christ's ministry to the world. It is a book about vocation, moving from an examination of some of the inter- and intra-personal barriers to effective ministry to an exploration of that inner relationship with God where ministry has its roots. Throughout what follows, I try to examine some of the ways in which the parish serves as a setting for ministry, paying particular attention to the ways in which a parish can become the kind of environment where ministry and solitude are experienced as one. One particularly important way of approaching this task is to develop the gift of discernment, referred to briefly in Chapter 1 and discussed more fully in Chapter 5. In Chapter 7 I try to spell out a contemporary theology of spirituality for "life in the world," using the idea of the Sabbath as a model. The Epilogue is quite frankly an apologetic for an expression of the Christian faith that is wholeheartedly in dialogue with the world. It is a plea for what might be called a "holy worldliness."

In a book entitled *Mutual Ministry,* written in 1977, I noted that unless there were major attitudinal and structural changes within the life of the church, the gains made toward the recovery of total ministry could well be lost. All that has happened in the years since then has only served to intensify my concern. My own vision, however, has changed. I have come to see more clearly that Christian ministry is born, not in activity, but in solitude. This book seeks to explore this thought.

I am indebted to all I have received from others that has helped me to write this book. In particular, I am grateful to Dean O. C. Edwards of Seabury-Western Theological Seminary for the invitation to give the 1980 Stewart Lectures, from which this book evolved. Other parts of the book were originally prepared for presentation at a conference on spiritual direction held at the Continuing Education Center of the Virginia Theological Seminary and at a conference on renewal and evangelism held in St. Louis. Throughout the past year, these initial reflections have been changed and expanded and presented at clergy conferences and retreats, where they have been discussed and further developed.

And finally, I would like to thank my colleague Alan Jones, who provided the impetus to getting these thoughts in print, and—once again—my good friend Earl Brill, of the College of Preachers in Washington, D.C., who made many helpful suggestions about how I could say what I wanted to say with more clarity. I am also indebted to Kate Treasure, who has helped me put these pages into their final form.

CHAPTER 1

A Renewed Sense of Ministry

Because he is bound to me in love,
therefore will I deliver him;
I will protect him, because he knows my Name.
Psalm 91:14

Down through the ages there have been times in which the
Holy Spirit has swept through the church with a particular
intensity. When that has happened, every aspect of the
church's life has been touched, as men and women have been
called to new levels of faith and degrees of commitment. There
are many who believe we are in such a period now. Such
optimism, however, needs to be tempered with caution. There
are, indeed, signs of renewal in the church, seen particularly in
a resurgence of concern for recovering that total ministry of
Christ's people that this book seeks to explore. But there is
also in the church tremendous resistance to change, and an
unwillingness to face the hard problems confronting the
church and the society in which we live. All too often
"renewal" has become a code word for what is really narcis-
sism thinly disguised as religious fervor. To speak the words of
renewal is not enough. The action of the Spirit demands that
we respond in ways that take seriously the rapidly widening
gap between the affluent and the poor both in our own
country and throughout the world. We are being called to re-
examine the very norms and structures by which the church
lives, lest what we say be denied by what we do. The Christian
Gospel calls us to nothing less than the radical transformation

of human life both personal and social. What is needed is a church so open to the new possibilities presented to it by the Spirit that Christians, by the very way they view the world, will be signs of the new age that is emerging.

The renewal of the church, by its very definition, involves the renewal of ministry. We worship a God who, in Paul's words to the Philippians, "emptied himself, taking the form of a servant" (2:7; RSV). God does not wait for us to seek him; he first seeks us. He is a God who acts, involving himself in every aspect of the human condition. Christian ministry reflects the nature of God himself, because it is through our reaching out, as instruments of God's love to others, that Jesus Christ is seen and known. The renewal of ministry involves not only a deeper awareness of our relationship to the Lord but also a renewed sense of what it means to share in Christ's ministry to the world.

A renewed sense of ministry involves both a new sense of mutuality that must exist between the clergy and the laity if the church is to be faithful to its task, and the realization that, for such mutuality actually to exist, there must be a theology of the church to undergird it. We are therefore seeing the emergence of a theology that understands the church not as a community gathered around a minister, but as a community of many ministries, each dependent on the other and all dependent on the Lord. If such a theology is to take root and grow, there are three issues which must be addressed. We must address the gap which continues to exist in many areas between the clergy and the laity. We must address what it means to be a "gifted" people. And we must address what it will mean for clergy and laity alike to develop a spiritual discipline that takes seriously the busy lives most people live and also take seriously what the Bible refers to as "the principalities and powers" of the world. I would like to look at the implications of these three issues for the life of the church in the world today.

The Gap Between Clergy and Laity

A gap between clergy and laity exists whenever a member of the laity or a member of the clergy feels that his or her own particular ministry is blocked or diminished by the ministry of the other. Sometimes the sense of diminishment can be very subtle, as when we are made to feel that our particular gifts are not really as important as gifts that are more dramatic or more obvious. Sometimes it is church structures themselves that produce the sense of diminishment—structures that limit our capacity for open communication and rapport. The way you view the gap between clergy and laity, of course, depends on your perspective. The clergy fault the laity for being unwilling to claim the ministries they have been given, and preferring to look to the ordained person to do the ministering for them. The laity fault the clergy for being unwilling to give up control. In an article in the Alban Institute's *Action Information,* Patricia Drake sharply criticizes the church (and the clergy) for their preoccupation with psychological concerns at the expense of other equally important areas of human experience. If as much time were given to supporting the ministries of those who are able to take initiative on their own as is given to those who are dependent on the initiative of others, she points out, the church would be a stronger institution. "The clergy are arrogant about what the world is about," Mrs. Drake writes. "They must learn to respect the complexity of the world and they must learn about it from those people who are working in it—not just the lame, the halt, and the blind."[1] This does not mean, of course, that the church should not be concerned with those in acute need, nor does it mean to deny the fact that leadership by its very nature often causes both separation and isolation, and often rightly so. What it does point to, however, is the gap that is formed, not as the result of courageous action or of differing function, but because of the breakdown of trust.

Trust, however, goes both ways. In the same issue of *Action*

Information in which the Drake article appeared, members of the clergy speak of such things as the lack of accountability on the part of many people who take on jobs and do not follow through; clerics also express their uneasiness (often well-founded) about people in strong leadership positions who can pull the church toward actions that are unfaithful and destructive. Because we do not talk openly about these things, the gap widens, and there occur needless insecurity, overdependence, conflict, and, most serious of all, the stifling of gifts.

In a study of its ecumenical doctor of ministry program, done several years ago by the Hartford Seminary Foundation, participating laypersons were asked to give their understanding of how the ordained person in the local church was to relate to the congregation at large. Prior to this study there had been a great deal of discussion about the meaning of a more mutual ministry between clergy and laity, a theme that the whole program was meant to underscore. In their responses, the laypersons identified five ways in which they saw the ordained person. (1) Some saw him as their private mentor with whom they enjoyed a close personal relationship. The way in which this relationship was nurtured and sustained seemed to be their primary criterion of measurement. (2) Another group identified the ordained person as the "shepherd of the flock"—he or she leads, and the people follow. (3) A third group viewed the pastor primarily as a "limited expert," competent to speak in clearly restricted areas, and resented when moved to speak about issues outside the accepted boundaries of those areas (normally, the areas understood as "religious"). (4) A fourth group clearly considered the cleric the "employee" of the congregation, functioning in the same way as the manager of any business enterprise and subject to the same criteria. (5) The fifth group was clearly the smallest among the hundred or so persons interviewed. This group viewed the ordained person as one called to enable the ministries of the congregation to be called forth and supported. They were in sympathy with the aims of the doctor of ministry program because they perceived that to be its emphasis. The others, especially those who saw the pastor as employee, were resistant in varying degrees to being told they had a ministry that they were called by the Spirit to claim. I was personally surprised at the diversity of this response (as well as its intensity), particularly when I reflected on the fact that all of the people responding were considered "active" church people. The response indicated just how much needs to be done.

As this study shows, the gap between clergy and laity is real. It is, in many cases, a theological as well as a psychological gap, and it is one that will not disappear without some real changes in both belief and practice. It is a gap that will be overcome only when a few people—some ordained and some not—begin to reach out to one another in new ways to seek what we hold in common. That will mean being willing to change those structures that limit or diminish any ministry of the church, and being willing to view the functions of ordained persons in new ways. Our task is not to diminish any order of ministry in the church, but rather to enhance to the fullest what God has given. We will know we have made progress when the quality of parish life is not judged by congregational size or affluence, but, instead, by the way clergy and laity support each other in the diverse ministries each has been given to do.

The Meaning of "Giftedness"

We are seeing in the church today a re-emergence of a theology of "giftedness." The recovery of the shared ministry given to us in baptism is directly related to our ability as a church to understand and claim the diversity of gifts that the Holy Spirit has given. In the First Epistle to the Corinthians, Paul makes a persuasive claim for the gifts that the Spirit bestows on those who share in the ministry of Christ. "I am always thanking God for you," he writes to that tiny group of Christians assembled in Corinth. "I thank him for his grace given to you in Christ Jesus. I thank him for all the enrichment that has come to you in Christ. You possess full knowledge and you can give full expression to it, because in you the evidence for the truth of Christ has found confirmation. There is indeed no single gift you lack.... It is God himself who called you to share in the life of his son Jesus Christ our Lord; and God keeps faith" (1:4-7, 9; NEB). This, to my mind, is one of the most hopeful promises in the New Testament. Paul is saying to this unexceptional group of Christians living in the city of Corinth that within their gathering all the gifts were present which God has given to his church. "There is indeed," he says, "no single gift you lack." Gifts of wisdom, administration, healing, teaching, discernment—they were all there, scattered throughout the body and residing in the most unexpected people. A gift is a quality of our Lord's life given to us by the Spirit for the building up of the church and for the manifestation of Christ in every setting in which we find ourselves. Sometimes these gifts are buried within us, unused, waiting to be discovered and called forth. Sometimes, however, gifts seem to be given quite unexpectedly, in order to meet particular circumstances—like suddenly knowing what to say when feeling inadequate and unable to speak. Some gifts are quite dramatic, but most are amazingly simple—like being able to listen or being able to offer support to another person in time of crisis. Some gifts stay with us a long time, others change as our lives change. Gifts, in whatever form they are given to us, are the substance of ministry. They begin with God's first gift to us all, the gift of ourselves. Elizabeth O'Connor has written:

> When I become aware of my own gifts and give my attention to communicating what is in me—my own truth as it were—I have the experience of growing toward wholeness. I am working out "God's chosen

purpose," and am no longer dependent on how others think and how they respond.... The teaching-preaching ministry of the church is to help a person discover the gifts he is to use in the creating of [his] life, in building the Church of Jesus Christ, and then finally, for his commissioning in the world so that he can be [in Isaiah's words] 'the repairer of the breach, the restorer of streets to dwell in.'[2]

One of the heresies that still persists in the contemporary church is the belief that the gifts necessary for the life of the church are centered in one person, and that person must be ordained. Priesthood is indeed a gift, and a very special gift, but it is only one of the gifts necessary for the fullness of the ministry. To my mind, one of the most exciting phenomena in the church today is the recovery of this sense of "giftedness" on the part of a large number of diverse people. We are discovering that we do indeed have evangelists, teachers, prophets, and healers in our midst, and they are beginning to discover what such gifts mean.

Having said this, however, allow me to say a word of caution. Giftedness is a mystery of the Spirit, and as a result there is a danger in being too specific about it. The claiming of a gift is the fruit of discernment—and discernment is our response to a nudge that gives us a hint that God intends us to use our life in a new and possibly more intentional way. We are never given a gift in isolation. It is always related to the community of faith, is always to be confirmed by the community of faith, and is always an expression of the Christ who dwells within us.

In the twelfth chapter of 1 Corinthians, Paul spells out his theology of giftedness. He speaks of gifts in quite concrete terms, reminding us of their infinite variety. And yet when he reaches the end of the list, he discounts everything he has said before. "And now," he says, "I will show you the best way of all":

I may speak in tongues of men or of angels, but if I am without love, I am a sounding gong or a clanging cymbal. I may have the gift of prophecy, and know every hidden truth; I may have faith strong enough to move mountains; but if I have no love, I am nothing. I may dole out all I possess, or even give my body to be burnt, but if I have no love, I am none the better.

Love is patient; love is kind and envies no one. Love is never boastful, nor conceited, nor rude; never selfish, not quick to take offence. Love keeps no score of wrongs; does not gloat over other men's sins, but delights in the truth. There is nothing love cannot face; there is no limit to its faith, its hope, and its endurance.

Love will never come to an end. Are there prophets? their work will be over. Are there tongues of ecstasy? they will cease. Is there knowledge? it will vanish away; for our knowledge and our prophecy alike are partial, and the partial vanishes when wholeness comes. When I was a child, my speech, my outlook, and my thoughts were all childish. When I grew up, I had finished with childish things. Now we see only puzzling reflections in a mirror, but then we shall see face to face. My knowledge now is partial; then it will be whole, like God's knowledge of me. In a word, there are three things that last for ever: faith, hope, and love; but the greatest of them all is love.   (1 Corinthians 13; NEB).

The ultimate gift of the Christian pilgrimage is love. It is a gift clearly related to faith and hope, but distinct in itself. To love another human being is to fulfill the potential of every other gift we have been given. To love is, in Paul's words, the summation of what it means to be a bearer of a spiritual gift, and the test of that gift's authenticity. When a gift is separated from its source, it becomes a distortion of what, in Christ, it was intended to be. Nothing is more destructive than loveless evangelism or loveless healing or any use of a gift so as only to enhance the prestige of the bearer. The exercising of a gift in love enhances and empowers the recipient. We decrease and the other increases that God alone may be glorified. Love cannot be earned, or bought, or coerced. It is a gift to be given away—the fruit of the intimacy that God offers to us in Christ. The source of all giftedness is the love of God. Although we experience this love through other people, we encounter it also in the stillness of our own being, like the water of a spring welling up within us.

When we talk in the church about claiming our gifts or calling forth the gifts of others as if this were a technique to be mastered, we are in danger of separating giftedness from its source. Each of us has been given an array of spiritual gifts, some known and some unknown. We will know how to express them fully as we know him who is their source. "In a word, there are three things that last for ever: faith, hope, and love; but the greatest of them all is love."

The Development of a Spiritual Discipline

Christian ministry is more than doing good. Ministry is an act of service performed either consciously or unconsciously in the name of Christ. Ministry is Jesus Christ expressing his life through us. It is born, therefore, not in activity, but in solitude, where through the Spirit we experience the power of life from within. No one becomes a "minister." Rather in trust we so open ourselves to the Spirit that Jesus Christ can express his ministry through us. Prayer and ministry, therefore, are indissoluable. In the stillness of meditative prayer we are confronted by God's loving claim upon us—the most intense intimacy a human being can experience. To know this intimacy we have only to let go. Instead of relying on our own initative, where we are in control, we discover that we are participating in what God has already initiated within us. As Henri Nouwen suggests in his beautiful little book *With Open*

Hands, the experience of God's love "demands a relationship in which you allow the other to enter into the very center of your person, allow him to speak there, allow him to touch the sensitive core of your being, and allow him to see so much that you would rather leave in darkness."[3] I both resist this intimacy and yearn for it at the same time; and yet, unless there is a regular time in my life for the cultivation of such intimacy, ministry becomes simply something else I am pledged to do in an already crowded life.

In his excellent book *Soul Friend,* Kenneth Leech suggests that the recovery of the gift of discernment might be the "most central thing happening in Christian spirituality today." "Discernment," he writes, "involves clarity of vision. . . . discerning, discriminating, judging between truth and falsehood. The recovery of the tradition of discernment involves in part the recovery of the unity of spirituality and moral and social action."[4]

Discernment is the gift that enables us to identify gifts in ourselves and in others. It is the gift of spiritual vision that enables us to see, if only for a moment, with the heart and mind of Christ. It is through the gift of discernment that we are able to perceive what God's will for us seems to be. Discernment is cultivated in silence and expressed in community. It is a gift that we desperately need to cultivate within the life of the church. It is, however, not a gimmick, but rather the fruit of conversion and profound inner discipline. As Paul writes to the Romans, "let your minds be remade and your whole nature thus transformed. Then you will be able to discern the will of God, and to know what is good, acceptable, and perfect" (12:2; NEB).

Discernment is that form of personal and communal prayer which seeks the guidance of the Spirit. It is also the gift that enables us to see the forces in the world that both blind us and hold us in bondage.

Several years ago, just before moving to New York, I went into a department store in the city I lived in to return a

Christmas gift that did not fit. The store was crowded with post-holiday bargain hunters. I, I said to myself, was not one of them. With firm resolve I returned my gift and headed for the door, threading my way between counters of merchandise, when suddenly I stopped. Something caught my eye and the process began. "That shirt is just what I need." ("But I have plenty of shirts," responded another voice) "After all, it's on sale." ("You are still spending money for something you don't need") And so it went. I bought the shirt, not because I needed it, but because at that particular moment I was in bondage to a spirit that pervades every aspect of our society. I was buying not out of need, but in response solely to the urge to buy. In this particular instance, the stakes were small, maybe even unimportant, but multiplied a thousandfold, my response involves a spiritual issue of profound consequence for the world we live in. It has been said that it is greed, more than anything else in today's world, that denies and hinders our interdependence and prevents us from understanding ourselves as a global community. The Asian thinker Kosuki Koyama has called it the "unclean spirit number one." And, as Elizabeth O'Connor has pointed out, when we agree with that statement it should not only be in condemnation of the world's greed, but in fear and trembling at our own.

"True spirituality," writes Kenneth Leech, "is not leisure time activity, a diversion from life. It is essentially subversion, and the test of its genuineness is practical. Discipleship involves a real transformation of character."[5] Christian ministry is Christ's life lived out in us. It involves a spirituality that girds us for battle against those principalities and powers which blind us to injustice and the suffering of others and ultimately opens us more deeply to God's claim upon our lives.

The Challenge Before Us

We are moving into a new era and we are laden with new challenges and new responsibilities. The evangelistic task is immense, but never was the world more ripe for harvest. The future of the world will be very much influenced both by the faithfulness of those decisions made by Christians in undramatic places and by their ability to proclaim the Gospel so that others can hear and see. We have an opportunity for a witness that the world needs desperately to see—a witness that manifests a vision of human community based on mutuality and support, an inner discipline that makes possible the recognition of the gifts we have been given, and a style of life based on a perception of simplicity and love as greater treasures than affluence and power. We have been given a ministry in our baptism—a ministry that is deepened and confirmed when in the stillness we hear the Lord speak his word to us and we dare to say yes.

CHAPTER 2

Mutuality and Maturity

Come now and look upon the works of the Lord,
what awesome things he has done on earth.
                                                    Psalm 46:9

Whenever church people talk about relations between the clergy and the laity, it is often to affirm one at the expense of the other. When we speak of the need for strong leadership among the clergy, that is often interpreted to mean that the laity will of necessity be diminished in their opportunities for leadership. Or when we talk of strong and articulate leadership among the laity, it is assumed that this of necessity will be a threat to the clergy. What is needed is a vision and a strategy that will take us beyond our rather limited view of what is possible in the church to a more realistic assessment of what might be. I believe deeply that the laity of the church are called by virtue of their baptism to share in the ministry of the Gospel. Whenever this ministry is diminished, the church is diminished. The word *laity* comes ultimately from the Greek word *laos* which means "the people." To speak of the ministry of the laity, therefore, is to speak of the ministry of the people of God exercised in every nook and cranny where Christian people live and work. *Laity* is an affirmative word, unlike the related *layman* or *layperson,* both of which suggest being less than expert and therefore beneath the "professional," which in the church is seen as the one who has been ordained. There are, of course, areas where the clergy, by virtue of their training and experience, do have a particular expertise. But there are other areas where the expertise rests with the laity and where the priest is the layperson. I for one would like to see the word *layperson* abolished altogether in referring to the ministry of the church, in order that we might emphasize the interdependence inherent in our baptism. It is far more accurate to say that John Jones or Mary Smith is a minister in St. Mark's parish, where William Gomez is the priest and pastor.

The point is, however, that until we begin to speak of ministry as something that is normative in the life of the church, it will continue to be seen as something that is highly specialized and normally "churchy" in its connotation.

To speak of total ministry in the church is to speak of a ministry of all of the baptized, each dependent on the gifts of the other. It is my conviction that strong and committed laity produce strong and committed priests. The reverse is also true. Strong and committed priests will produce strong and committed laity. I use the word *strong* here not in the sense of being dominant, but as a way of describing an inner strength that does not depend on being in control in order to feel affirmed. This inner strength is the essence of vocation. It is the product of a growing intimacy with the Spirit—an intimacy that frees us to let go of our need to control, and enables us to be a source of strength for others.

The Significance of Ordination

The ordained ministry within the life of the church is given to the church in order to maintain the Gospel tradition from one generation to another and to insure within the Christian community a sign of Christ's presence. The office of priest is a continued reminder to the church that it is fundamentally an intercessory community sharing in the sacrifice of Christ on behalf of the world. In the same way the office of bishop is a reminder to the church that it is fundamentally an apostolic community called to proclaim the Gospel in every corner of the earth. The office of deacon is a reminder of our fundamental servanthood—a reminder that to feed the hungry and to heal the sick, to set at liberty those who are oppressed, is an expression of who we are because it speaks of who Jesus was and continues to be in our midst. The sacrament of ordination seeks to bring into sharp focus through a specific office within the church those fundamental elements within our Lord's ministry that in a more general way are shared by the church-at-large. Because some people are bishops, some are priests, and some are deacons in the church of Jesus Christ, all of us are reminded of what is fundamental to our calling—to be evangelists, to be intercessors, and to be the servants of Christ on behalf of those for whom nobody speaks.[1]

The gap between clergy and laity which in our time is so common and so destructive had its origins in the early part of the fourth century in what has sometimes been referred to as the "Constantinian Captivity." When the emperor Constantine was converted to Christianity, the Christian church moved from being a persecuted minority to being a privileged majority. This made it possible for the church to engage the culture in new and significant ways; it also caused the church to reflect more and more the culture of which it was a part. The clearly delineated hierarchy and elaborate ceremonial of the empire were reflected more and more in the life and structure of the Christian community, producing what was for all intents and purposes a priestly caste. It is easy, of course, from the perspective of the twentieth century to see this only in its negative aspects. To do so would be not only unfair but inaccurate, since the Spirit was clearly as much at work in the fourth century as it is in our own. The accommodation that took place, however, did intensify the separation between the ordained and the general ministry of the church to such an extent that even the lay preachers of St. Dominic and St. Francis and the call to a priesthood of all believers (articulated in the Reformation of the sixteenth century) could not fully overcome it.

The vocation of the priest within the life of the Christian community is, and always has been, a special calling that is shaped by a particular combination of gifts. The ordained ministry demands a life of dedication and self-sacrifice that demands respect when that life is so lived and calls forth justifiable concern when it is not. I would add to these qualities the capacity to live as a "liminal person,"[2] which Urban Holmes speaks of as the calling to live on the boundary between structure and anti-structure, between the world of order and reason and the world of intuition and imagination, in a way that can manifest to others the multidimensional nature of our spiritual pilgrimage. The significance of ordination, therefore, is not that it makes someone better or even fundamentally different, but that it offers to the church a living symbol of its own identity. When the power of this symbol is able to empower others, then it truly reflects its source. For this to happen, the one who is set apart by the community to be the tradition-bearer and the symbol of Christ's presence must also experience herself or himself as an equal part of the community, dependent on the gifts of others for carrying out the ministry ordination implies. It is difficult to live in the tension between "set apartness" and authentic mutuality. It can only be accomplished when, by the grace of God, ministry in all of its diversity is seen not as the privilege of one but as the vocation of all who are baptized into the ministry of Christ.

The Necessity of Interdependence

Given the state of the world in which we live and our responsibility for it, the Christian church can no longer live by the shortsighted vision of ministry that has characterized its life in the past. The tasks that are before us are too far-reaching. We are being called to make those changes within our common life which will both produce and insure a degree of mutuality between the clergy and the laity that we have not experienced in a long, long time. The difficulties inherent in such changes are profoundly theological, and yet they are generally articulated in very pragmatic ways. As a sales representative for a hardware manufacturer put it, "I like to think of myself as a person with a pretty strong ego who meets people easily. But how, I ask you, am I supposed to feel equal with a man who is the focus of all my 'feelings' of dependence on God?" Or, in another vein, the question is raised by a woman who is trying to maintain a home while working at a very demanding and responsible job. "How," she asks, "am I supposed to have the same feeling of responsibility for my parish church, as a part-time participant, as my parish priest for whom this is a full-time occupation, and for which she is paid, to boot?"

These questions point to a host of issues that must be explored. The clergy and the laity have different institutional commitments and limited time. A gap exists between an educated clergy and a laity who are generally less informed in matters of theology and ecclesiology, but often more informed in the secular disciplines. And there are the difficulties created by an unwritten expectation that all conform to a spiritual discipline that is monastic in its origin, and often incompatible with the active life in which most people are engaged in the world. Our struggle to build a more mutual and interdependent ministry within the church will only develop as questions of this kind are addressed from the varying perspectives which each of us brings. Our first step is to build within the church the kind of trust that will allow these questions to be asked— and answered. Such trust will only emerge when all who share in the ministry of Christ engage each other, not only in terms of their institutional commitments, but in the shared experience of solitude where our common commitment to Jesus Christ finds its roots. Solitude of this sort can never be imposed. It must be mutually sought and mutually shared by each according to the gifts he or she has been given.

A Vision of Christian Maturity

Visions are the windows through which we view the world. They shape our expectations of what is to be and give us structures for moving into the future. What is needed in the church today is a vision of ministry that encompasses all of life and empowers men and women to bear witness to the presence of Christ at every point where human beings interact with one another. To live by such a vision implies that everything we do and everything we say—indeed, everything we are—is or should be an expression of the ministry we have been given in Christ. It is not a question of task but of identity. *Ministry* is the word used by Christians to describe the way in which they live out the implications of their baptism. The question, therefore, is not whether or not we have a ministry, but where it lies and how it may be realized. For some it will mean grappling with a business decision in the light of what is understood to be God's purpose for the world. For another it will mean standing as an advocate for a fellow employee in a time of trouble. For another it will mean preparing for a ministry to the sick and shut-in. For another it will mean celebrating the Eucharist on behalf of others with whom ministry is shared. Ministry is a question of intention. It involves what we understand to be the meaning and purpose of our lives. For some are called to be prophets, some teachers, some administrators, some healers, some priests, some evangelists, and some bearers of the presence of Christ in ways that are unassuming and hardly noticed. As was noted in the preceding chapter, a new vision of ministry will emerge as we come to believe that we really are a "gifted" people as the New Testament proclaims, and that the fulfillment of our lives is directly related to expressing these unique gifts. Such an emphasis, I believe, will produce a new understanding of what constitutes Christian maturity in the life of the church. Let me suggest five signs of this maturity, realizing, of course, that maturity is expressed in different ways in different people.

First of all, growth in ministry must involve growth in self-awareness. Self-awareness makes it possible not only to discern the gifts one has been given but also to identify the ways in which these gifts can be most authentically expressed. Self-awareness involves sensitivity to one's impact on others as well as an ability to receive criticism and use it for one's own growth. Self-awareness implies a sense of one's own finiteness and, in Christian terms, profound dependence on the infinite forgiveness of God. I can look most honestly at myself when I have come to understand that my ultimate justification does not depend on what others think of me, but on what God has done for me in Jesus Christ. Christian maturity emerges from the tension between this realization and the realization that we are indeed dependent on others for much of what we need to know about ourselves.

Secondly, Christian maturity is reflected in an increasing sense of wonder and awe. One of the paradoxes of the Christian life is that the more deeply we come to experience God, the more aware we are of how limited our knowledge of him actually is. As Paul says, "we see through a glass, darkly" (1 Corinthians 13:13; KJV). Christian maturity involves a high tolerance for ambiguity and paradox and a lessened need for certainty. The more we come to know of the world, the more aware we are of the mystery and awesomeness of what lies behind what is at best only partly seen. This sense of wonder allows us to open doors rather than close them in our relation with others. It allows us to value questions as highly as we value the answers that these questions imply.

Thirdly, Christian maturity involves commitment to a disciplined pattern of nurturing the life in Christ. Such a pattern involves a life rhythm that moves easily between solitude and action. It will involve an increasing knowledge of scripture as a means of understanding one's own identity. Such knowledge comes from within us as we ponder and listen to the words of scripture in solitude as well as with others. A growing awareness of what it means to live in Christ involves a growing awareness of the meaning of Christian community. A sign of Christian maturity is the realization of what it means to be a part of an intercessory community where we participate in the liturgy of the church ("the work of the people") not only out of our own need, but on behalf of others. Christian maturity is reflected in a life lived consciously in the presence of God.

Fourthly, Christian maturity involves a growing capacity to respond to the pain of others, including the pain of persons very different from ourselves. The economist Kenneth Boulding has said that "it is always easier to get people to pursue the interesting than the important."[3] Christian maturity involves in human terms the ability to discern this difference and to direct one's energy toward solving problems rather than perpetuating them. Christian maturity is seen in the capacity of one person to walk in the shoes of another. It is reflected in our commitment to justice and mercy, particularly in situations where self-interest makes issues of justice and mercy hard to perceive.

Finally, Christian maturity is reflected in our capacity for joy. For the Christian, all life is a gift. We are the recipients of a love that will not let go. To recognize this fact is to experience that sense of joy which comes from profound gratitude for a love that is sheer gift. Christian joy is more than a good feeling. It is an ability to appreciate the gifts we see in others. It is a response to life that overcomes cynicism and allows for hope, even in the midst of darkness. We can sense joy in others not by the giddiness of their behavior, but by the way their joy empowers us.

This vision of ministry will be realized when the life of the church matures and deepens beyond its present level. Too much of our energy is spent on peripheral concerns. The Christian life involves growth in Christ. It involves becoming so open to his presence that his life is reflected in ours. As this happens, maturity develops. Christian maturity, therefore, has little to do with whether we are ordained or not. It is the common quest that involves us all. We will discover our mutuality not in our differences, but in the solidarity that comes in the recognition of a common pilgrimage.

CHAPTER 3

Power, Achievement, and Affiliation

Our help is in the name of the Lord,
the maker of heaven and earth
Psalm 124:8

One of the realities of parish life is that the ordained person
has a great deal of influence in either blocking or enhancing
the ministries of others. As the designated spiritual leader of
the congregation, the priest or pastor by his or her encouragement and support can create an environment where ministry is
able to flourish once the vision has been grasped by others.
Unfortunately the opposite may be true. Since it takes more
time and effort to develop ministry than to perform it oneself,
the priest can block the development of ministry either by
outright opposition or, as is generally the case, by benign
neglect. I would like to explore the role of the ordained person
in the development of ministry within the life of the parish,
paying particular attention to some of the things that get in
the way. It is my growing conviction that when the clergy
themselves become the major stumbling block to the development of total ministry, it is generally not by intention; it is
rather the result of a combination of many factors inherent in
the structure of most congregations. When things don't work
the way we want them to, rather than finding someone to
blame, it might be well for us to examine together (as a
congregation) the norms that shape parish life and the
attitudes and convictions that lie behind them. For it is
generally at this point that change needs to take place.

Genuine mutuality within the ministry of the Christian church will only occur as the gifts of both laity and clergy are enhanced to their fullest. It is interesting to note that in the great bulk of literature on the development of religious community there is consistent mention of the one who is set apart by the community to represent in some way its continuity with the past. Whether called guru or shaman, medicine man or priest, a symbolic person seems to be necessary to a religious community as a source of continuity and unity. Within the Christian tradition, those who have been set apart by ordination are fundamentally the tradition-bearers of the community, embodying both symbolically and functionally that ultimate mystery by which the community understands itself. Tradition-bearers, therefore, are not peripheral to the Christian community, but rather are psychologically, functionally, and theologically necessary for the church to be itself. The ministry of the total congregation is blocked when the symbolic power inherent in the office of priest is used either as a way of manipulating persons to do what the holder of that office wants or as a shield to hide his or her own vulnerability. When we talk about blocks to ministry, therefore, we are not asking for the diminution of the symbolic power of ordination; we are arguing for greater clarity and authenticity in its expression.

In his work on the nature of effective leadership David McLelland suggests that there are three basic needs present in any organization.[1] They are the need for power, for achievement, and for affiliation. When met creatively, these needs can become assets. When unmet, they serve to prevent effective leadership from emerging. In considering the role of the ordained person in the life of the congregation, the identification of these needs is particularly helpful. When the needs for power, achievement, and affiliation are dealt with openly, and structures are established by which they may be met in normative fashion, genuine mutuality among all who share in the ministry of Christ may indeed become far more apparent than it is now.

Power

Power is a word we use to decribe the energy we need to take desired action or accomplish desired goals. In the Bible the words for power are used many times, but with a progressive concern for their spiritual content. In New Testament times this concern culminates in the primary association of power with the personality of God himself. Paul speaks of Jesus as "the power of God" (1 Corinthians 1:24) and calls us to a faith not based on human wisdom but on the power that comes from God. The same word, *dynamis,* is used in speaking of Pentecost—"you will receive power when the Holy Spirit comes upon you" (Acts 1:8; NEB)—referring to the power given to the church to bear witness to the Gospel. In all of these references, it is clear that the word *power* is always associated with God's power. It becomes demonic only when separated from its source.

In the person of Jesus, however, power takes on a particular dimension. In Jesus Christ, God the Creator, the All-Powerful One, emptied himself of all claim to power and assumed the form of a servant. On the cross his powerlessness becomes the sign of his triumph. Power is a gift of God to be used for the empowerment of others. It is a source of life only when it is given away. Power becomes a problem in the church when it is viewed as a commodity that comes from the top down, and must be guarded and controlled in the same fashion if it is to be exercised responsibly. The result of Pentecost was a new, radical understanding of community, different from anything the world had known. By the time of Constantine much of this radical vision had been lost, only to emerge with a vengeance at various times in history. The recovery of ministry is directly related to the recovery of a more biblical understanding of power. All power derives from God. It is given to the community for the accomplishment of its mission, a mission that involves giving power away for the empowerment of others. Effective leadership does indeed involve the use of power, but it is power that must ultimately be tested by the power of the cross.

Whether we like it or not, the notion that, despite all words to the contrary, power is invested in the clergy is built into the very structure of the church and confirmed by centuries of tradition. This notion is strengthened by the symbolic power inherent in our understanding of ordination itself. When power is ascribed to some designated element within the Christian community, rather than to the community at large, it becomes focused on the *institution* of the church rather than on the *mystery* that the church and its ministry embody. The result is the creation of a separate class that operates by a separate set of norms and by a special wisdom not available to others. As one member of the laity has commented rather poignantly, "When I criticize my priest for making a mess of things, there is a dull fear invoked in me that I can't readily explain. It is not that I think he is God, but that he hooks things in me that are both mysterious and threatening." The power is real but is perceived as a threat because it is associated with the priest as an institutional representative who is beyond criticism, rather than as a fallible and human instrument of power that only has meaning when it is given away.

When the use of power in the church is misunderstood or misdirected, a number of blocks seem to emerge and tend to become part of established tradition. To begin with, in the eyes of many people, the priest is seen as the one who exercises ministry *in the place of* the congregation. He or she is hired to act on behalf of others because the priest alone has the power necessary to do the job. And a corollary to this is the unwillingness on the part of many to hold the priest account-able by normal standards of accountability. When what the priest says or does is contrary to the expectation of the congregation, the dissatisfaction is generally not dealt with openly; it is expressed by the exercise of undefined counter-power. People quietly withdraw their support. The issue for the priest when this occurs is a larger issue than that of loss of power. It can seem to be a loss of identity, and the priest's natural response to that crisis may well be to tighten whatever reins of control are available to him or her.

I have been in many groups lately that were dominated by clerics who talked too much. They were not even aware of what they were doing, but nevertheless went on and on, insensitive to the impact they were having on others. When I experience this same thing happening in myself, I can be sure of one thing: there is something going on in me that is making me uneasy about questions of identity and power. Leadership and the use of power, you see, are not merely a matter of preference. They are a matter of theology.

To build new structures in the church that contribute to the mutual ministry of all who are baptized in Christ will involve some radical re-thinking of both our attitudes as a church and the means by which we carry out our mission. There is no way to do this without moving more consciously from our limited hierarchical model of church life to what can be more clearly perceived as a collegium. The ministry of the bishop must be redefined to allow him (or her, as the case may someday be) to function more fully as a teacher and missionary among equals, leading by virtue of his personhood and the particular gifts associated with that first apostolic company. Persons called to the ordained ministry need to be assisted in making a choice between priesthood and diaconate, so that the diaconate may emerge as a ministry of servanthood with an integrity of its own, and not merely a stepping-stone to the priesthood and thereby (as we say) a lesser order.

In the local congregation all possible support must be given to developing its understanding of the church as a community of many ministers rather than a community gathered around *the* minister. I see this going hand in hand with the cultivation of the gift of discernment so that in every congregation men and women are raised up who are seen to possess this gift in a recognizable way. Their task, whether they are one or two or one hundred in number, will be to exercise the ministry of the shepherd—helping others discover and act on the gifts they have been given. The United Church of Christ and the Baptist churches come close to this idea in the office of deacon, which for them is a lay office carrying with it both prestige and power. The function of deacons in these churches, unlike the functions of vestrymen or board members in other groups, is not linked primarily to administration, but to a more direct ministry to individuals in need. Perhaps the diaconate, as it is understood historically in the Episcopal Church, has implicit in it a model for ministry that is as clearly defined and empowered as that of warden and vestry member.

Structural changes are very much needed. We need to establish clear models for various forms of ministry both in the church and in the world at large. Once established, these ministries must be empowered by every means available to us. I know of one congregation that elects its vestry by pulling names from a hat. Every name in the congregation goes into that hat—if the person has agreed ahead of time to the statement adopted by the parish of what is expected of a vestry member. That statement, incidentally, requires a clear commitment to ministry. Such a move is a radical departure from established procedure, but in this particular instance it produced a new vision of participation and ministry because it took seriously the question of power and how power is expressed through the particular gifts we have been given.

The temptation to use power for our own ends is subtle and pervasive. It is, as we see in the temptation of Jesus, a temptation that strikes at the heart of vocation and could—if yielded to—ultimately cut us off from the root that sustains all true vocation. "A man with grace is a man who has been emptied, who stands impoverished before God, who has nothing of which he can boast," writes Johannes Metz. "This poverty, then, is not just another virtue—one among many. It is a necessary ingredient in any authentic Christian attitude toward life."[2] The feeling of powerlessness and the need to control are fundamentally spiritual issues. We are set free to use the power we have been given when we discover in the depth of our being that we are, indeed, powerless and that it is only in this condition that we encounter the One who for our sakes gave up all claims to power that he might meet us where we are. To discover this is to discover the true meaning of ministry.

Achievement

The way power is used in the church affects us all. It affects our motivation and the degree of commitment we have to the ministries we have been given. Our need for a sense of achievement, however, is of equal importance. It is almost impossible to sustain anything if it does not contribute to our sense of accomplishment, even if that sense of accomplishment is tied up with nothing more than survival. Everyone needs the sense of being able to accomplish what he or she sets out to do. The need to achieve stimulates our creativity and expands our imagination. But because achievement is often hard to measure, its presence or absence can be hard to judge. And its absence can contribute to feelings of inadequacy and self-depreciation that can be paralyzing in their effect. The rolls of parishes are cluttered with the names of people who have drifted away simply because they felt that their efforts on behalf of others in the parish went unrecognized and unappreciated.

The need for a sense of achievement is as real for the parish priest as it is for members of the congregation—but with some subtle differences. There lingers in our mythology the image of the selfless priest who has never, for one moment, worried about accomplishing anything, his life being in the Lord's hands. The myth is a paradoxical one. When we experience this level of intimacy with God, there is a sense in which our achievement needs are indeed fulfilled, but because so few of us experience this kind of intimacy in any sustained way, we may also come to feel we have not measured up at all.

Added to this is the difficulty of measuring achievement in the life of the parish. How does one measure the achievement involved in hours spent with a dying parishioner or in leading a service of worship? There is so much that is intangible in parish life—it is hard to measure. I remember so well the feelings of frustration and restlessness I used to feel in my parish ministry. I learned to resolve them by making parish calls at the end of the afternoon. I could say to myself that I had visited eight homes and made contact with twelve people, and I felt better. This difficulty is often compounded by other factors—low clergy salaries and the absence of any clearly recognizable system of recognition and promotion comparable to that in the secular world, for instance.

In the parish ministry an unfulfilled or blunted sense of achievement can produce two serious blocks to mutuality in the life of the church. The first is what I would call a "Lone Ranger" style of leadership and the second, for lack of a better term, limited vision. A Lone Ranger mentality enhances a sense of competitiveness. Limited vision makes it almost impossible to recognize and affirm any ministry that does not directly meet the church's institutional needs, even when such a ministry is clearly an expression of the church's mission.

There is a time in every expression of ministry when we must stand alone. Being alone in this way is the price of leadership, a price that can be particularly heavy in the ordained ministry. The priest by nature of his or her calling is a sign of contradiction. He is both the reconciler and the bearer of the prophetic Word—the bearer of both the peace of Christ and the sword of Christ. To discover in the solitude of prayer the resources necessary to be apart is to discover the freedom that only Christ can give. Such separation, however, is quite different from that suggested by the image of the Lone Ranger. The former is freely chosen; the latter emerges out of a need to be safe at any cost. Unfortunately, all too many clerics learn from their seminary experience not what it means to stand alone as a sign of grace, but how to remain separate in order to minimize risk. The idea is to remain relatively cool and detached until a need arises; then we sweep in by ourselves to solve the problem. This style of action says, "I can work best by myself," and it stems from a fear that if I reveal my real lack of achievement to a potential colleague, the truth will be known and my deficiencies will be found out. Or else, if I reveal my successes, even in a modest way, I will not be believed—or if I am believed, I will be rejected. Gore Vidal wrote that "everytime a friend succeeds I die a little." No doubt we all have had feelings like that, but it does not take much imagination to see what it can mean to the life of the church when these feelings are not dealt with.

Unresolved feelings of lack of achievement cause compulsive overwork, competitiveness with peers, and a chronic unease with the kind of collegiality that mutuality demands. They make it difficult to affirm ministries outside the life of the parish because our institutional needs for success are so strong. Everyone who has ever served in the parish ministry knows the feeling of ambiguity that comes when the superintendent of your church school comes to tell you she is resigning to begin a creative ecumenical ministry concerned with improving the quality of education in the local schools. Our theological impulse wants to affirm this person and set her free, but our institutional impulse hates the very thought of letting go. This fact alone makes a strong case for having persons other than the rector of a parish exercise the ministries of discernment mentioned earlier—ministries concerned with helping people discover and act on their gifts within and beyond the parish framework.

In responding creatively to achievement needs within parish life, however, we find ourselves faced with other problems. For instance, one must consider how the clergy are trained. Seminary education, with its subtle emphasis on competition and individual rewards, needs to take into consideration the ways in which people can be helped to work more collegially in settings where there is sufficient trust to allow failures and successes to be shared. On a diocesan or judicatory level, we need to develop systems of recognition and affirmation that are appropriate to the vocation of ministry but allow alternatives to the unwritten assumption that achievement means being called to a larger church. Achievement means using your gifts to the fullest, and the setting for ministry depends largely on the unique set of gifts each of us has to offer. In the parish we will respond to the issue of achievement when we see that we should—and must—have standards of accountability that will apply to all who are engaged in ministry—clergy and laity alike. Although some of the works of ministry cannot be evaluated, some clearly can. When evaluation is used not as a method of judgment, but as a stimulus to growth, it can be of immeasurable benefit in helping the whole parish understand where it is going and how well it is realizing what it has set out to do.

But there is another side to the question of achievement—one that is more than structural and yet is basic to any resolution. In our innermost depth our need for achievement can never be satisfied by what we can measure. In the parish ministry there is always more to be done than we can do. A sense of worth is the fruit of transformation. It is through faith in Jesus Christ, and his ultimate achievement in his cross and resurrection, that our lives are ultimately justified and our worth assured. To accept this as the central reality of our lives is the most critical spiritual concern that confronts us. It is, in fact, the ultimate concern that lies at the heart of our profession of faith.

Affiliation

The third and final category of need to which McLelland refers is what he calls *affiliation*. Affiliation refers to our need to belong, our need to be a part of something larger than ourselves. It is the psychological base of our experience of intimacy, for it is the principal need that draws us to other people. At one level our need for affiliation can be met simply by participating with others in a common task. At the level of intimacy, more is required. We experience intimacy with another person when our need for self-protection is at a minimum and when the barriers that normally separate us are at least momentarily overcome. Intimacy is the gift of grace. At its deepest level it occurs when we are most fully open to the presence of God and thus through him to another human being.

In the conclusion of his book *The Wounded Healer,* Henri Nouwen makes a penetrating comment about the relation between intimacy and ministry.

> When the imitation of Christ does not mean to live a life like Christ, but to live your life as authentically as Christ lived his, then there are many ways and forms in which a man [or woman] can be a Christian. The minister [or priest] is the one who can make this search for authenticity possible, not by standing on the side as a neutral screen or an impartial observer, but as an articulate witness of Christ, who puts his [or her] own search at the disposal of others. This hospitality requires that the minister [or priest] know where he stands and whom he stands for, but it also requires that he allow others to enter his life, come close to him and ask him how their lives connect with his.[3]

Nouwen is speaking of what is ultimately involved if genuine mutuality between clergy and laity is to be achieved and sustained. To speak of mutual ministry is to bear witness to the fact that the ministry of one Christian is incomplete without that of others. We are speaking of a ministry that calls us into genuine intimacy with other human beings at a deep spiritual level.

If we are serious about the way we are present to others, we need to take a hard look at some of the dynamics of parish life that work against the very things we profess. There is much in parish life that works against genuine intimacy and leads us to settle for superficial encounter. Obviously, we cannot be intimate with everyone all the time. It is neither possible nor appropriate. The issue is whether we are able to be genuinely intimate with anyone when the opportunity really does present itself. During my five years of working with laypersons at the Hartford Seminary Foundation, I heard, over and over again, expressions of despair on the part of the active laity over what they perceived to be the emotional unavailability of the clergy. We talk a lot about risk, but many perceive us as low riskers ourselves. The clergy talk about openness and what it means to be present to others, but all too often they are perceived as persons with a very high need to guard their vulnerability and maintain control. Obviously, this description is sometimes mistaken, and of course this is not a problem unique to the clergy; but it rings true enough in my own life for me to take it seriously.

Our need for affiliation and intimacy is brought into balance when our need for approval is lessened and our capacity for risk is heightened. At one level the need for affirmation and approval is healthy and necessary, but at another level nothing can be more destructive of our ability to share mutuality with others. We can tell a lot about ourselves by the way we say yes and say no, and whom we say them to.

In 1963 I left the parish ministry to work as director of education for the Episcopal Diocese of Washington. I had been the rector of a rapidly growing suburban congregation in the South, one composed largely of people my own age. When I began my new ministry in Washington, I found myself becoming increasingly depressed. I had expected the sense of displacement that comes with a move, but this was more than that. It had to do, I soon discovered, with the emotional withdrawal of the almost continuous affirmation I had been used to receiving. (It is my experience that in a parish, no matter how badly things are going, there is always someone who will tell the priest he or she is doing well.) Thus I learned at first hand how difficult it is when affirmation is not received, and why we will go to such pains to sustain it. But to be so dependent on a climate of continuous affirmation not only limits our capacity to deal openly with conflict, it also causes us to overwork or to make demands on family and friends that they are unable to meet. And if we are not careful, it causes those of us who are parish priests to be less than honest in our dealings with parishioners and fellow clerics, and can be destructive of our relationships with the people we love the most.

Closely related to the problem of unhealthy dependence, of course, is what we generally refer to as counter-dependence— the need to fight and create distance from the source of our dependence in ways that are compulsive rather than free. When we are caught in the dependent-counter-dependent bind—even in small and seemingly unimportant ways—there can be no intimacy or mutuality. Intimacy involves owning our vulnerability and being open to the vulnerability of others. In a very real sense intimacy involves losing our lives in order to find them again at a deeper level. One of the difficulties of parish life is that we experience moments of great intimacy, only to have it suddenly taken away (which is usually the way it should be). It took me, as a parish priest, a long time to understand why I often found wedding receptions so difficult. It was because I had been so intimately connected with the couple while preparing them for marriage that it was a shock to discover I was no longer needed after the ceremony. I had done my job, and although I could rejoice in this, it was also a cause for pain.

Most of us in the priesthood learn to bear the pain of loneliness that intimacy invariably produces, learning how to maintain an appropriate distance from people. This distancing, however, when unchecked, can become a way of life in itself. Like overdependence, it is a sign that our needs for affiliation and intimacy are unresolved and more painful than we care to admit. Nothing can have greater effect on our homelife, our marriage, and our relationship to God.

Externally, we resolve our need for affiliation and belonging by solid structures of support. In most of us these sources of support vary in kind and in distance, but if they are to be helpful, they must be cultivated and sustained. Internally, our need for belonging brings us face to face with our Lord himself and the quality of our relationship to him. I am more and more convinced that the reason we of the clergy have so much difficulty with sustained prayer and contemplation is not lack of time—though time is required—but fear of intimacy. Intimacy is born and nurtured in solitude. To know what it means to cry, "Abba, Father," is to know what it means to be vulnerable, but free.

We can say all we want to about the recovery of the ministry of the laity and about the ministry of clergy and laity together, but the fact still remains that unless the clergy are themselves convinced and serious enough to let it happen, they can, within the life of the parish, effectively block what the Spirit begins. Our task is to mobilize men and women, each with his or her unique gifts, to share in Christ's healing ministry to the world. If changes are not made to sustain what the Holy Spirit has once again begun, we will have lost a critical oportunity at a critical time. The way we work with our need for power and achievement and affiliation in the life of the church is certainly not the whole answer, but it will determine to a great degree the quality of our contribution to this greater task—the participation of the church in the ministry of the Lord.

CHAPTER 4

The Parish as a Setting for Ministry

The earth is the Lord's and all that is in it,
the world and all who dwell therein.
Psalm 24:1

"One of the major tasks facing the Church," writes Bernard Cooke, "is the development of a theology of vocation wherein we can determine what ministries are needed and which should be discarded."[1] When we look at the church as a whole, we must accept the fact that we are a long way from this kind of understanding. Cooke is speaking out of a vision of the church as a community of many ministries, continually in flux in response to the challenges presented by the world. The vision, however, is not an impractical one. Every congregation has had to wrestle with what to do with groups or committees which have long outlived their reason for being. And every community has had to face situations where it has been unable to address a crisis simply because financial resources and people were tied up in already-existing organizations—organizations that, because of their longevity, often demand a loyalty far beyond actual need. There are, indeed, obvious examples of organizations and groups in which permanence and continuity are essential, but there is an equal need for the kind of flexibility that will allow for a ministry to be shaped in accordance with a specific need rather than having to find a need to fit the ministry. The vocational question, therefore, is not "What are we going to do now that we are together?" but rather, "What is the need around which Christian community should form for the exercise of ministry?"

In their provocative book *The Management of Ministry,* James Anderson and Ezra Jones suggest that if a parish is serious about preparing persons for ministry, it must begin by evaluating its effectiveness in a new way. The church, they point out, must gauge its success not by the number of activities taking place in its institutional building, or by the number of participants or the number served, but "by the quality of lives redeemed and the characteristics of the social milieu where these lives are lived."[2] Until we see this as our task—a task that includes the quality of family life in our community, the problems faced by the elderly and unemployed, the pace at which people live, the integrity of the business and government enterprise, the way one group interacts with another, to name just a few—our understanding of ministry is limited and our motivation for claiming our gifts is diffuse and confused. The importance of what Anderson and Jones are saying is the emphasis it places on the quality of ministry in the "scattered" church and the fact that it measures the ministry of the "gathered" church according to this standard, and not the other way around. Our task, therefore, is to try to see that the response we make to every situation in which we find ourselves has the capacity to alter that situation for good or for ill. The issue for the Christian, therefore, is not whether or not to "take on a ministry," but rather how our lives can be so sensitive to the movement of the Spirit in all that we do, that the gifts we have been given may be used in behalf of others. That is why the question of ministry can never be seen solely in terms of activity or organization. It has to do fundamentally with our theology of vocation. How, then, can the parish church begin to create a climate (or sustain that climate where it already exists) that will make this question of vocation paramount?

Ministry and Vocation

As we have affirmed again and again, ministry is not primarily an activity, but the fundamental expression of one's life in Christ. We do not invite people to claim their ministry, therefore, by giving them a job to do or by trying to reach them through a high-powered recruitment program. We try instead to help them find the roots of their vocation as baptized persons called to share in the ministry of Jesus Christ.

Several years ago the Alban Institute in Washington, D.C., published a very interesting study by Jean Haldane on the ways people understand and find support for what were defined as their "spiritual pilgrimages."[3] Ms Haldane interviewed a number of people, and discovered that for most of them there was a clear separation between what they understood to be their "spiritual pilgrimage" and their participation in the life of the church. As best they could identify them, spiritual growth was nurtured by things they read and by special groups or relationships, not necessarily related to the church. They noted that significant spiritual growth often occurred in times of crisis. The organized church, on the other hand, although often indirectly related to the nurturing process, was seen not primarily as a source of spiritual growth but as the place that met their need for "belonging." It was a place where socialization was seen as a greater priority than spiritual nurture or mission.

If Ms Haldane's findings are correct (and they are substantiated by many similar studies), they would suggest that any intentional effort to deepen a sense of vocation must take seriously the issue of belonging, and must also develop an approach to spiritual growth that is not dependent on specific programs, but that rather cultivates an environment in which spiritual growth in its broadest sense can be deepened and sustained. The people least likely to respond to programs of spiritual development—to prayer groups and retreats—are as important as those who do, but they must be reached in different ways. Vocation is rooted in prayer. It is the response with our lives to what we discern as God's purpose for us. There are many ways in which this discernment goes on— sometimes quite intentionally, sometimes quite by accident. The task of the congregation, therefore, if it is to become a community of many ministries, is to find a variety of ways to deepen what is already going on.

I have heard it said that in the fourteenth century the form of greeting that people used when they encountered each other in the market or on the street was not "How are you?" as we might ask today, but rather, "Is it well with your soul?" The contrast says a great deal about the environment in which we live. In its root meaning, our contemporary form of greeting reflects a concern for health; the ancient form reflects a concern for vocation. We cannot change the environment of an entire culture (at least not overnight), but we can change the environment of parish life so that we more nearly live what our vision proclaims.

The Parish as Environment

Just recently my wife gave me a copy of a book by May Sarton called *Journal of a Solitude*. She had been very much moved by it and felt I would be, too. Reading this book, therefore, had a particular significance for me. One passage in particular struck me because it spoke so clearly to the question of environment. May Sarton writes:

> A good piece by Auden in the *Times*. I read it while eating a hot dog at the kitchen counter and felt happy. His theme is that we are losing two precious qualities, the ability to laugh heartily and the ability to pray, a plea for carnival and for prayer, the conscious thumbing of the nose at death. I suppose that the only prayer—reached only *after* all pleas for grace or for some specific gift have been uttered and laid aside—is, "Give me to be in your presence."

And she continues:

> Simone Weil says, "Absolute attention is prayer." And
> the more I have thought about this over the years, the
> truer it is for me.... Something [in life] is "given," and
> perhaps that something is always a reality *outside* the
> self. We are aware of God only when we cease to be
> aware of ourselves, not in the negative sense of denying
> the self, but in the sense of losing self in admiration and
> joy.[4]

As I thought about the ministry of the local congregation
both as a gathered and as a scattered community, those two
words of Auden's that caught May Sarton's attention seemed
to me to be the key to what a parish can be and, indeed, must
be, if it is to take ministry seriously. What greater gift could a
parish have than to contain within it people committed to
keeping alive the spirit of carnival and that of prayer. And
what greater witness can we make to the world than to keep
alive those two qualities that Auden suggests we are in danger
of losing. Let us look then at what these two qualities—the
spirit of carnival and the spirit of prayer—might mean in
creating an environment in which vocation to ministry is
nurtured and sustained.

The Spirit of Carnival

When I think about the spirit of carnival a number of things
come to mind. Auden defines the word as the ability to laugh
heartily—even at oneself. When I think about how much
energy we waste in the parish worrying about little things, how
serious we become over petty concerns, I realize what an
important quality that is. In a parish I served some years ago
there was a lady who delighted in handing me notes about
what, she thought, was wrong with the parish just as I was
about to begin the morning service. A ministry of carnival in a
parish would counteract the spirit that moved this lady; it

would highlight the issues that ought to concern us, and make light of the petty issues that so easily come to seem central.

Carnival suggests to me joy in belonging, the capacity to celebrate our common life and our common faith. Every parish needs to be gratefully aware of serendipity, to have occasions when the unexpected gifts in its midst are celebrated and offered. Some time ago I had the privilege of leading a retreat for the Companions of the Holy Cross, a remarkable group of women, from all over the United States, who have bound themselves together by a common rule of prayer and service to support one another in living out the implications of their baptism. A highlight of this retreat was what was called a serendipity evening, a time when Companions could share with one another their unique gifts. One of the Companions, then well into her eighties, had for many years been a dancer and teacher of dance. As the evening drew to a close, she arose to make her offering. Her movements were slow and cautious, testing muscles long unused and stiff with age. But as she moved, there was a beauty it would be impossible to describe, a beauty that reflected the power of a disciplined life offered to God. It was an occasion I shall never forget.

In Christ there is a joy in belonging that needs to be lifted up and celebrated lest it be lost. Such occasions can be as simple as a parish meal or as elaborate as a public festival. The point is that vocation is nourished in belonging. In a very thoughtful booklet entitled *Going Public,* Parker Palmer speaks of the responsibility of the Church for the public realm.

> We have lost the private–public balance in our time. Today we live at the extreme suggested by the root meaning of the word "private": to be deprived of a place in public life.... The church has a vital role to play in restoring the balance, in bringing people from private into public life, for the Church itself spans the two realms.... The God who speaks in the silence of our private lives also calls us into public solidarity with others.[5]

Going public is a fruit of the spirit of carnival as it celebrates the presence of God in all of life and offers up the wonder and the diversity—and the tragedy—of the world for which Christ died. Finally, carnival suggests to me the spirit of abandonment, a word that is central to the spiritual life. Abandonment involves the capacity to give oneself away for the sake of another, to trust utterly in the providence of God. We are so cautious in so much we do that we lose the opportunity to stand for what is different from the world around us. There are enough incidents of injustice and need around us to occupy a lifetime—and to some of them we will only respond if someone is able to carry the day with, "It's crazy, but let's try it." As I observe some of the exciting and notable expressions of mission within the life of the church, I realize that they began just this way, in the spirit of carnival. As I reflect on the world we live in, and its increasing scarcity and imbalance, I wonder who in the Western world will lead the way in creating a totally new life-style for us all. It will take people with the spirit of abandonment, people who can let go easily for the sake of a greater value. When the spirit of carnival is alive in a parish, new ministries can emerge and flourish, for then our vision is not confined to a place but encompasses a world, and is limited only by our capacity to take in what God places before us.

The Spirit of Prayer

Prayer is a sister to carnival, since aside from its most serious side, prayer also manifests joyfulness and laughter—especially a capacity to laugh at oneself. There have been times when I have come to God preoccupied with myself and have felt as if I heard God laugh—and it helped me to laugh as well. But a ministry of prayer obviously involves more than this. It involves a life of intercession, quiet reflection, and conversation with the Lord. It also involves creating an environment in the life of the parish where prayer is seen as normative.

One of the problems that most parishes face is the idea that prayer is the activity of only a certain group of people. When you extend an invitation for people to participate in a prayer group, you can just about predict who will respond. There are obviously many reasons for this: a fear of being too personal, feelings of inadequacy—even guilt—about prayer, the sense that prayer is one's private business, or the plain fact that so many people know so little about prayer that they are afraid to begin. All these, and many more reasons, tend to make people hesitant to take the first steps. Underneath all this, however, is a deeper problem. The environment we experience in most parishes runs counter to what we say we believe. Instead of being caught up in a rhythm that moves between solitude and action (what I like to refer to as a Sabbath rhythm), we experience parish life primarily as activity. Since for many people, ministry is equated with the life of the parish, it is seen as an activity added to an already crowded list of activities, most of which are important and useful. We will never see Christian ministry for what it is intended to be until it is separated from mere activity and is seen as the expression of one's whole life. I am more and more convinced that this connection will not be made until parish life itself embodies this same spirit.

If we are going to deepen the spiritual life of the congregation we need to take seriously the environment in which parish life is experienced. As I dream about what could be done (and often *is* done), I think of such things as the use of silence—in worship (certainly after the scripture is read), before meetings, in pastoral situations. Not a mere moment of silence, mind you, but a period long enough for silence to settle in. I think of seeking to create a rhythm that balances every notable activity with an equal time of quiet, be it a retreat or a silent time within the life of the parish while normal events continue to take place. The idea would be to establish a rhythm in which people could experience the spirit of prayer without having to talk about it.

The establishment of such a rhythm would involve paying particular attention to what people are asked to do. It would mean suggesting to some people who are especially active in the life of the parish that they spend a period of time in other ways, whether with their families or simply with themselves. If a sense of vocation is to be deepened, we must have time to address the question, "Is it well with our souls?" A desperately needed ministry is one that will help raise this question over lunch tables and in casual conversation until it permeates everything we do. The frenzied pace of activity by which most of us live is destroying the meaning of life. It affects family life and the life of society as a whole. We will not change the perceptions people have about the life of the Spirit by formal education alone. We will only change perceptions when we take seriously how we use people (or *mis*-use them) and how we use the time we have been given.

To cultivate within the life of the parish the spirit of carnival and the spirit of prayer is to provide an environment that takes seriously the diversity in people's lives. It affirms the ministry of the "scattered" as well as the "gathered" people of God. But even more important, it acknowledges that the motivation for ministry is born not in activity but in solitude. Christian ministry does, indeed, involve "doing," for ministry involves service. This service is a way of expressing the gifts we have been given through the Spirit, but this root of ministry is found in another place where the emphasis is not so much on "doing" as on "being." A parish that is attuned to this can point to the things that are ultimately important, not only by what it says, but by the way it lives.

CHAPTER 5

Developing the Gift
of Discernment

*When my spirit languishes within me, you know my path;
in the way wherein I walk they have hidden a trap for me.*
Psalm 142:3

Not long ago on a seminary campus an incident took place that illustrates one of the most important spiritual dilemmas of our time. The incident involved a number of people of various Christian denominations, who were participating in a continuing education event dealing with the church's response to the larger community. The conference had been given a very controversial case study and asked to decide, along denominational lines, how they would respond. The groups met separately and then reported back to the total conference. Summarized rather briefly, the results were these: the United Church of Christ group reported that they would appoint a task force to work out a strategy to be voted on by the congregation; the Episcopal group announced that they would present the controversy to their vestry and ask for a decision; the Roman Catholic group announced that they would present the problem to their bishop for a ruling on how they were to proceed, and so it went. Finally, after much discussion, a black Baptist pastor of a rapidly growing store-front congregation stood up to make his report. "I don't understand where you all are coming from with all your talk about committees, and strategies and task forces," he said. "In our church I would call all the deacons together and we would lock ourselves in a room and we would stay there praying until the answer came." Everyone laughed, but it was nervous laughter. For in the silence of our hearts we were all musing over the disturbing possibility that we had been told something we very much needed to hear. The storefront pastor had been talking about the gift of discernment and its place in the life of the church. It is a gift that the New Testament talks about frequently, but in our organization-minded church of today, discernment seems strangely out of place.

As we noted earlier, discernment is a word used to describe our inner vision. It is a gift of the Spirit that makes it possible for men and women to perceive what God's will for them seems to be. Discernment, therefore, is a gift given to the whole church, to both clergy and laity alike, and it is dependent on the collective wisdom of the whole church for its testing and verification. If we are to respond seriously to the unique gifts given to the church for its ministry, we are talking about discernment. For it is through the gift of discernment that we are able to identify gifts in ourselves and in others. If we are to respond seriously to the movements within the church calling us to a more disciplined spiritual life, we are again talking about the gift of discernment. For growth in the Spirit involves both our ability to see where the Spirit is leading us and our capacity to identify the presence of evil that stands in the way. Discernment is the gift of prophetic vision that moves Christian spirituality from sentiment to reality.

Discernment and the New Testament

The word *discernment* is related to the Greek word *diakrino,* which means "I decide" or "I discriminate." In association with several other words, it refers to the power given us by the Spirit to perceive what in fact is God's will for us as individuals and for the world as a whole. When Jesus was asked by the Pharisees and the Sadducees to give them a sign from heaven, he refused, on the grounds that they would be unable to interpret the sign even if given it. Although they can look at the sky and see if a storm is coming, they are not able to "interpret [Greek, *diakrein*] the signs of the times" (Matthew 16:3; NEB). To do so implies a special gift that had not yet been given, a gift that the church later understood to be a fruit of Pentecost.

On a personal level, discernment involves being able to glimpse what God intends for our lives, to test through experience what his will seems to be. Such a gift is cultivated from within and is the fruit of our relationship to Christ. In his Epistle to the Romans, Paul makes the connection between conversion and discernment very clear. "Do not be conformed to this world," he writes, "but be transformed by the renewal of your mind, that you may prove what is the will of God, what is good and acceptable and perfect" (12:2; RSV). The Greek word, *dokimazo,* that the Revised Standard Version of the Bible translates as "prove" is translated in the New English Bible as "discern." It means literally to "distinguish by testing," a gift given to the Christian believer through his relationship to Christ.

But discernment in New Testament usage is more than a personal gift related to growth in the Spirit. It is the gift given to the church for calling forth the many other gifts bestowed upon the body of believers and the gift that enables the church—both the whole church and its individual members—to distinguish between what is good and what is evil. "There are varieties of gifts," Paul writes, "but the same Spirit.... To each is given the manifestation of the Spirit for the common good. To one is given through the Spirit the utterance of wisdom, and to another the utterance of knowledge according to the same Spirit, to another faith by the same Spirit, to another gifts of healing by the one Spirit, to another the working of miracles, to another prophecy, to another the ability to distinguish [*diakrino*] between spirits" (1 Corinthians

12:4, 8–10; RSV. See also Hebrews 5:14). Here discernment is seen as the political gift par excellence. It is the gift given to the church to unmask the principalities and powers—the forces that permeate and distort the institutions and customs that constitute human society. Discernment is the gift given to us so that in Christ we might confront evil face to face.

The Personal Dimension

When a man or women prays, "Thy kingdom come, thy will be done," he or she is presupposing the direct action of God in our day-to-day experience. God does not predetermine the outcome of our lives, but he does act in the world, wooing us into relationship with him. To say that God is love is to affirm that there is "a purposeful quality running through the whole creation,"[1] seeking by the persuasive energy of love to establish that kingdom on earth in which God's purpose for the world is fulfilled. Since we are part of God's purpose, it follows that every decisive moment in our lives must contain the possibility of our cooperating with the ongoing thrust of God's love or blocking that thrust, either by deliberate disobedience or by distorted and limited vision. The gift of discernment makes it possible for us to see in the midst of day-to-day events the direction in which God seeks to take us.

Discernment is more than human intuition, although it is related to it. We speak of being able to discern God's will when our natural intuition is so open to the prompting of the Spirit that it is literally transformed by it. My own decision to come to my present ministry, for instance, was a discerned decision. At the time, I was faced with two possibilities, in addition to the very real possibility of staying where I was. For several weeks I prayed that I might be led to do what best accorded with the direction God had already established in my life. I prayed especially that the power of my own ego needs might be minimized. As I approached the deadline for the decision, I wrote out in my journal the pros and cons of the possibilities before me, checking those pros and cons with a close friend to determine how realistic they were. There was a point in this process at which I experienced a new readiness to listen that had not been present before. And so I listened. My prayer was simply, "Lord, show me the way," and he did. The answer came not as a thunderbolt but as a quiet unfolding. After a restless night, I woke knowing what my decision would be, and I made it. Although there is no way that I can say with absolute certainty that this was God's will, it felt, and continues to feel, right. My experience exemplifies one way in which the gift of discernment can become a part of our spiritual pilgrimage.

Discernment also involves confrontation with evil. It is the gift that enables us to break the power that evil can have over our lives. To understand discernment in this way, it is necessary to accept the fact that there is, despite all our protestations to the contrary, an evil force at work in the universe, one that is independent of ourselves. Evil is the distortion of good. It is energy cut off from the purposes for which it was intended and is, therefore, fundamentally destructive of life. I know the power of evil in my own life when I find myself giving in to pressures within me that run contrary to both what I believe and what I most want for myself. Or I see this power magnified in the transformation of a crowd into a mob. Evil is the word we use to describe that energy that, though once created by God, has been cut off from the central thrust of the universe and runs madly toward its own—and our—destruction.

One way to discern personally the power of evil is to determine the degree to which a particular expression of evil is "at home" in our lives. We are all continually faced with one temptation after another in the experience of living. Some temptations, however, have a way of moving in to the center of our psyches until they become as familiar to us as a picture on the wall. Before long we have lost both the ability to see what has happened to us and the ability to resist.

I have a friend who for a long and anguished period of time

was engaged in an affair with a woman with whom he worked. My friend was married and the father of four children. He came to see me one evening in a desperate attempt to find the strength to break off the affair, which—he knew full well—would ultimately mean the destruction of his marriage.

"At first," he said, "the relationship was life-giving. Ann and I enjoyed being with each other because there was a sense of spontaneity and freedom that neither of us had ever known before. But before long, this all changed. It is as if I am locked in a vise and unable to act. I see my willpower and my resolve gradually fading away."

The evil with which my friend was dealing was his own inability to make a moral choice. He could not say yes to his wife or to the woman with whom he was having an affair. He was, in New Testament language, under the bondage of sin.

The gift of discernment involves both self-knowledge and an active and informed conscience, for it is the gift by which we differentiate the power of life from the power of death. In discerning the presence of evil in our lives, we can be enormously helped by a wise and trusted spiritual companion or director. Such a person can keep us from becoming scrupulous on the one hand, or simply naive on the other. It is a relationship that only has meaning, however, when we become serious about the awful reality and subtle destructiveness of sin. "If we say we have no sin, we deceive ourselves, and the truth is not in us," writes the author of the First Epistle of John. "If we confess our sins, he is faithful and just, and will forgive our sins and cleanse us from all unrighteousness" (1:8-9; RSV). When evil is unmasked and seen for what it is, it loses its power over us, and we are no longer in bondage to it. This, Christians believe, is the redemptive work of Christ.

The Corporate Dimension

In 1976 an Episcopal parish in Missouri was faced with a momentous decision. A member of the congregation had died and, to everyone's surprise, left this relatively small church a trust fund just short of a million dollars. The income alone was more than twice the existing parish budget. As the congregation wrestled with the implications of the bequest, the central question became very clear. They phrased it quite simply: "What does God want us to do with this money?" And as they explored further, people saw the need to get a clearer sense of "what God wants to do with the church" and "how He wants to use the individuals that make up its membership." None of these where small questions.

At the suggestion of the bishop of the diocese, leaders in the parish consulted Father George Schemel, S.J., the director of the Jesuit Center for Spiritual Growth, in Wernersville, Pennsylvania, who agreed to come to the parish and train the congregation in discernment. In 1977 three parish retreats were held. The first focused on the quality of prayer life within the parish, the second on the specifics of the Jesuit method of discernment, and the third on the process of discernment itself as the parish sought God's guidance in how to use the income from the endowment. In reflecting on the experience, Howard Park, the rector of the parish, notes that the process led the parish to a clearer sense of its mission and resulted in short retreats' becoming a regular part of the ongoing life of the parish. More important still, the gift of discernment had become a critical element in the vestry's decision-making process—not as something unusual, but as a normative part of parish experience.

In an article entitled "Communal Discernment: Reflections on Experience,"[2] Father John Futrell describes one way of applying the Ignatian method of discernment to a communal setting. The process begins with a series of exercises aimed at achieving a common identity and purpose. Individual faith journeys are shared, a statement of common agreement is prepared and affirmed, and a common commitment is made to carrying out the decisions reached through communal discernment.

Next comes the process of deliberation. When a concern is brought to the surface and agreed upon as important enough to warrant such commitment, all possible evidence is gathered and made available to all who will be engaged in the deliberation. Then the process begins. In brief, it includes the following steps:

1. A period of meditation and prayer seeking openness to and guidance from the Spirit.
2. The sharing of "cons," as each person reports the reasons against moving in a particular direction that he personally discerns.
3. A period of prayer allowing time to reflect on the serious- ness of the "cons" that have been shared.
4. A sharing of "pros," as each person reports his own personal discernment. If no consensus emerges, the process continues.
5. A period of prayer allowing time for reflection upon step 4.
6. An effort to sort out and weigh the reasons behind the pros and cons, recording those reasons so that they are available to all, and to discern communally, in the light of what has been listed, the choices to which the community is called by God. In commenting on this aspect of the process, Father Futrell writes, "If the Holy Spirit is working through the second time of election, and if the conditions of authentic communal discernment have been fulfilled [i.e. if there is genuine openness to the Spirit], the decision should be made clear, and confirmation should be experienced unani- mously through shared deep peace....finding God to- gether."[3]
7. A concluding prayer of thanksgiving and the reaffirmation of corporate commitment to carrying out the decision.

At first glance, such a process seems unduly long for the everyday decisions that take place within the life of a parish. That would depend, of course, on the time given to each step.

It could involve a month or an evening, depending on the seriousness of the issue. What is important, however, is the spirit behind the process, and the conviction that it is indeed possible for a group of people who believe that God is active in the world to move beyond personal prejudice and self-interest, however enlightened, to a new level of awareness that has been shaped and transformed by the presence of the Holy Spirit. For a community to live this way clearly differentiates it from the society of which it is a part and restores to the church a level of spiritual integrity that is very much absent in the world in which we live.

Discerning the Principalities and Powers

Discernment is a prophetic gift given to the church for its battle against evil. "We have the prophetic word made more sure," writes the author of 2 Peter. "You will do well to pay attention to this as to a lamp shining in a dark place" (1:19; RSV). As we all know, that is not an easy task. As a human institution, the church itself is part of the problem.

In referring to the presence of evil in the world, the writers of the New Testament had a way of speaking that, in the light of contemporary experience, appears remarkably insightful. They saw evil not only as an individual matter (if every individual were good, the world would become good as a natural result), but as a problem of creation itself. When the Bible speaks of the Fall it is referring not simply to individual sin, but to the way in which sin is present in the structures individuals have erected. In referring to these structures, the New Testament speaks of the "principalities and powers" of the universe. Because these principalities and powers exist in a fallen world, they are estranged from God (like the rest of creation) and have taken on both a personality and an authority all their own. As William Stringfellow points out:

> The very array of names and titles in biblical usage for
> the principalities and powers is some indication of the

scope and significance of the subject for human beings. And if some of these seem quaint, transposed into contemporary language they lose quaintness and the principalities become recognizable and all too familiar: They include all institutions, all ideologies, all images, all movements, all causes, all corporations, all bureaucracies, all traditions, all methods and routines, all conglomerates, all races, all nations, all idols.[4]

The church, like all institutions, is a principality. At the moment it claims an identity and a destiny apart from the identity and destiny given it by God, it becomes a demonic power at emnity with the purpose for which it was created. At the moment a government, or a cause, or a tradition becomes an end in itself, unable to view itself as a part of a larger plan involving the whole created order, it is, at that moment of its blindness, in bondage to what the New Testament refers to as "the powers of darkness" that, by their very nature, are headed for ultimate destruction.

In the fifth chapter of the Gospel According to Mark this insight into the corporate nature of evil is illustrated with dramatic vividness. During his Galilean ministry, Jesus crossed over the Sea of Galilee to a barren section of country known as the country of the Gerasenes. There he was met immediately by a deranged man who had been living among the tombs. The man was in such a state of maniacal frenzy that he had broken the chains that had bound him and was cutting himself with stones. Jesus saw the man as one possessed by an unclean spirit and began to call the demonic spirit out from within him, only to discover that he was possessed by a number of spirits speaking with one voice. ("My name is Legion," said the spirits to Jesus.) Jesus called these spirits out of the man and he was healed, but the spirits moved immediately into a herd of pigs, which rushed over the edge of a cliff and were drowned (5:1-17).

The point the Gospel makes is quite clear and quite perceptive. Evil cannot reside in a vacuum, it must be embodied within some form that will give it life. In a human being, it had to struggle for mastery. In a herd of pigs, where there was no resistance, it sought its own destruction, and, undoubtedly, the destruction of the pigs as well.

M. M. Thomas, an Indian theologian, argues that all authentic Christian spirituality must be a "spirituality for combat."[5] He means by this that authentic Christian spirituality must do battle not only with personal evil, but with the principalities and powers that shape the world in which we live. It is a never-ending warfare, in which the price is high and, because of the blinding nature of self-interest, distinctions subtle. The weapon we have been given is the gift of discernment, to be used prayerfully and carefully as we seek to discern God's presence and direction in the world around us. On the cross Jesus confronted the principalities and powers in all their fury: the government, the church, racial prejudice, movements for liberation and movements for the protection of the status quo—all were aligned against him. By the power of his love, he unmasked them and rendered them powerless to destroy him. In cosmic terms, we are engaged in the same struggle, although there is one significant difference. We are part of the struggle as ones who also share in the victory. In Jesus Christ, we are given the power of life, which alone can conquer death. The gift of discernment is an expression of the redemptive power of God in the world. It is a sign that his kingdom will ultimately come and his will be done, on earth as in heaven. The word to us, therefore, is "Be alert, be wakeful," for we do not know "when the moment comes" (Mark 13:33; NEB).

CHAPTER 6

Inner Growth and Outer Change

Teach me to do what pleases you, for you are my God;
let your good Spirit lead me on level ground.

Psalm 143:10

Christian ministry and the quest for solitude are indissoluble
companions. It is in solitude that we experience the ministry
of Jesus Christ within, and it is in service to the world around
us that we express this ministry without. Growth in the Spirit
occurs through the living out of this dual motion. As our
relationship to the Lord begins to deepen, so also is our life
transformed. Inner growth, if it is authentic, produces outer
change.

Unfortunately, our futile efforts to fill our lives with activity
and things leave us no time or space to nurture the relationships Jesus offers. To be alert involves friendship with
solitude, a knowledge of that center within ourselves where
intimacy with God is deepest and we can see the world—if
only momentarily—through the eyes of Christ. Growth in the
Spirit, therefore, requires the time and effort and openness to
become a person of serious and consistent prayer. Many
people have found help by developing spiritual companion-
ships, which can supply both support and direction along the
way. A spiritual companion is a very special person in the
Christian life. He or she is a "soul friend" to whom we can talk
about our growth in the Spirit. If such a person is experienced
in the life of prayer, he or she can provide very valuable
assistance and direction. As we begin to experience change in

our lives, it becomes especially important to reflect on the change in the light of that vision which calls us forward. In a spiritual companionship we seek constantly to discern whether our inner growth is indeed a response to the working of the Spirit or is simply the extension of our own ego.

The idea of spiritual growth is deeply rooted in scripture. In the Sermon on the Mount, Jesus issued a call to perfection that has deeply influenced our understanding of the Christian life (Matthew 5:48). In his letter to the Ephesians, Paul echoes this call in his exhortation to be "imitators of God" (5:1; RSV), as in his letter to the Colossians he speaks of presenting everyone as a person "mature in Christ" (1:28; RSV). It is in the Epistle to the Hebrews, however, that the idea of progress in the spiritual life is most clearly articulated: "Therefore, since we are surrounded by so great a cloud of witnesses," we read, "let us also lay aside every weight, and sin which clings so closely, and let us run with perseverance the race that is set before us, looking to Jesus the pioneer and perfecter of our faith" (12:1-2; RSV). It is here that we get a clear sense that growing in Christ involves a sense of movement, a sense of self-discipline, but also the promise of support from others who have also run the race and in so doing obtained the prize.

The question that has plagued the church down through the centuries, however, has to do with the way we have interpreted this call to ongoing spiritual growth. For some it has meant a life of solitude in the desert. For others, it has involved a life of strict obedience in one of the great religious communities that have emerged as men and women have sought holiness. For many of the Protestant reformers of the sixteenth century, the very idea that there could be spiritual progress through obedience to a rule was anathema; they considered it one more instance of the erroneous idea that salvation could be won by "works." They preferred instead to emphasize the sanctification that comes as the free gift of the Spirit.

There is, of course, danger in any vision of the spiritual life that suggests that if we follow a particular formula, we can be assured that we will progress onward and upward according to some set pattern. Experience teaches us that this simply is not true. The spiritual life is a life lived in response to the Spirit, and the Spirit of God cannot be programmed or bound. Growth in holiness is the work of the Spirit in us, and it has no predetermined pattern. Salvation is a gift won for us in the death and resurrection of Jesus Christ. It is in him and through him that our worth is affirmed. Spiritual growth never involves winning this affirmation but is always a response to it. I seek to grow in Christ, not to win his approval, but in response to his love.

In my own experience spiritual growth has more to do with accomplishing tasks than reaching stages. These tasks reoccur and deepen as we grow in the Spirit, but they are there. Six such tasks seem to be central to growth in Christ. They involve a spiritual awakening, the quest for clarity, change of behavior, a reoccurring sense of the absence of God, compassion, and an increased simplicity in one's life. Spiritual growth involves responding to these inner tasks at greater depths and with more long-lasting consistency.

Awakening

An experience of spiritual awakening is an inner task to the degree that we respond consciously to the movement of the Spirit within us. One of the great illustrations of what happens when we are awakened by the Spirit is found in the eighth chapter of the Gospel According to Mark. As Jesus arrives at Bethsaida a blind man is brought to him to be healed. Jesus takes the man by the hand and leads him out of the village, where he proceeds to put saliva on the blind man's eyes. "Do you see anything?" Jesus asks. And the man responds, "I see men; but they look like trees, walking." And again Jesus touches the man's eyes and, we are told, the man begins to see everything clearly (8:22–26; RSV).

As the blind man encounters Jesus, the first stirrings of faith are awakened in him. He can see, but not clearly. His perception is distorted. But the encounter continues, and at last he begins to see. For St. Paul, the awakening is more dramatic still. On the road to Damascus he is confronted by the risen Christ and experiences a total reordering of his life. Relationship to Jesus Christ becomes the dominant and overwhelming concern of his life.

Awakening ultimately involves conversion. It might begin with a nudge, with the experience of thirst for the holy, or with the realization of what it means to surrender one's life to God. Whenever the experience of awakening occurs, it involves the dissolving of the boundaries of the world we have known and a glimpse of a new world where God stands at the center. Jesus referred to this world as the Kingdom of God.

For someone caught up in an awakening experience, several things are important. Affirmation and support, of course, are central. There is also a need for an ongoing experience of community, where there can be further exploration and reflection. This is a time when selected reading is particularly important and when the guided study of scripture needs to be suggested and encouraged. But it is important to remember that the awakening task of spiritual growth is not a once-and-for-all experience. It occurs again and again in different forms and with different intensity as new worlds are opened to us and we begin to see the world around us with new eyes. We respond to the sense of awakening within us through serious prayer and through the struggle to let go some of the inner controls that keep God at a distance. The task of awakening is to honor the stirrings of the Spirit that we find within us.

Clarity

To be awakened by the movement of the Spirit, however, does not necessarily imply that we know where those stirrings come from or to whom our response should be directed. When I first began to take the practice of meditation seriously,

I was fascinated by the variety of experiences and methods that were available to me. I found myself in a world of many wonders. The task of clarity involves being very clear about whom it is we seek. The goal of the Christian life is to live in such an intimate and ongoing relationship to Jesus Christ that his life is seen through our own. St. Paul writes to the church in Colossae, "As therefore you received Christ Jesus the Lord, so live in Him, rooted and built up in Him and established in the faith" (Colossians 2:6–7; RSV).

The spiritual task of clarity, therefore, involves both study and reflection. Since we always see the Lord "through a glass, darkly," we are always engaged in this task at different levels of experience. "Whom do you seek?" is the question that needs to be asked as we pursue this task. What perceptions do we need to let go of as we draw closer to the Lord? How can our prayer be more focused and more intentional? A sign that we are working on this task would be a sense of confusion about prayer or a restlessness that makes it difficult to bring our prayer into focus. Clarity of spirit, of course, is ultimately a gift. It is the gift of inner sight ("insight"), by which we see anew through the eyes of Christ. It is this understanding that lies behind T. S. Eliot's much-quoted line from "Little Gidding": "the end of all our exploring/ Will be to arrive where we started/ And know the place for the first time."[1]

Behavioral Change

There is no way in which we can be drawn into intimate relationship with Jesus Christ without at the same time becoming aware of our inadequate and distorted reflection of the life he offers to us. At the root of our lives there is a deep separation between us and God, a separation that manifests itself in an inflated sense of self (or its opposite, a diminished sense of self) and a consequent need to control what we think of as our own destiny. We call this separation sin. Its only ultimate remedy is repentance and the acceptance of that divine forgiveness from which a new life can be forged.

Choosing to live one's life in Christ is in a profound sense not only a difficult choice, but a narrow choice because it demands that we say no to those things that get in the way.

"Enter by the narrow gate," Jesus told his disciples, "for the gate is wide and the way is easy, that leads to destruction, and those who enter by it are many.... [But] the gate is narrow and the way is hard, that leads to life, and those who find it are few." To which he adds, "You will know them by their fruits" (Matthew 7:13–14, 20; RSV). These are not words that we generally associate with the spiritual life, but they are words that are essential to any serious attempt to enter into combat with those forces that erode human freedom and ultimately destroy human life. The spiritual life is particularly susceptible to sentimentality and lack of consistency. We can withdraw into our "center" as if it were another world, substituting the "feeling" of encounter with God for the encounter itself. There are many people involved in the practice of meditation whose day-to-day lives are a moral shambles. Ultimately, we must ask ourselves in what way the practice of prayer makes a difference in the way we live. Kosuki Koyama writes that "the presence or absence of acts of self-denial must be a fundamental criterion for the life inspired by religious teaching."[2] He notes that although the practice of self-denial is fundamental in all of the great world religions, it has been suppressed in contemporary Christian practice, at great cost. The issue, of course, is not self-denial for its own sake, but the self-denial that emerges out of concern for those who have less than we and a desire to share more authentically in Christ's ministry to the world. The practice of self-denial at its deepest level is an expression of the solidarity that is the first of Christ's actions in us.

In working on the spiritual task of behavioral change, our aim is to achieve greater congruence between what we say we believe and the way we live. The task of a spiritual guide is not to lay down a new law but to enable a person to live the life that best reflects the image of Christ that is within him. We can help best by pointing out inconsistencies and areas for possible growth, knowing full well that similar inconsistencies and lack of congruence are present in us as well. The sacrament of Reconciliation can be of great assistance in this area because it brings us face to face with the specifics of sin in the context of God's infinite love and forgiveness. Although there are times when a spiritual director is not the best choice for a confessor, more often than not, when the same person serves in both capacities, it adds to the depth of the relationship. In Christ we are given the freedom to be who we were created to be in him. Change, if it is to be authentic, must be seen in this context and not imposed from without. It is the fruit of transformation within.

Absence

There is no one who has worked at the discipline of prayer for any length of time who has not experienced a sense of God's absence. For Christians the ultimate expression of this absence comes from the cross itself, when in one brief agonizing moment there comes from the lips of Jesus a cry of desolation: "Eli, Eli, lama sabachthani?" "My God, my God, why hast thou forsaken me?" (Matthew 27:46; RSV).

Some moments are ultimately unexplainable. They are moments when, in the providence of God, we are left to walk alone, seemingly in utter isolation. For most of us experiences of this sort come when the pain of grief or the anxiety of worry or sickness passes like a cloud between us and God and he is cut off from our experience. To St. John of the Cross, such an experience came not as the result of any external circumstance, but as the fruit of prayer itself. He came to see his Dark Night of the Soul as a necessary element of the experience of intimacy that God offers.

In his classic rules for discernment, St. Ignatius Loyola gives three reasons why God may permit desolation. The first is our own resistance or negligence. The second two are closely related and are considerably more subtle. "God may try us to test our worth" or to teach us "that it is not within our power to acquire" genuine consolation, which is purely "a gift and grace of God our Lord."[3]

Everyone who prays is familiar with the problem of resistance or negligence. We become bored or restless when nothing much seems to be happening, and we give up. Our spiritual well is dry and, no matter how hard we try, even the thirst we once knew seems no longer there. What is needed is encouragement and support, not to try harder, but probably to try less, letting the Spirit move within us until the flow is experienced again.

But sometimes, lying beneath this turning away, there is a deeper problem. It is possible that our prayer has brought us closer to God than we were prepared for. It is in dealing with this reality that we are, in St. Ignatius' words, "tested," not in the sense of being put on trial, but in the sense that steel is tested by fire—that is, purified and made strong. When in our aloneness God seems utterly absent, and we are forced to let go simply because all attempts to summon him or even to recall a past feeling that we associate with his presence fail, there is nothing to do but wait.

What we see on the cross is not that God is absent, but that even in the experience of his absence, he is present, but hidden from our sight. The role of the spiritual director assisting someone in dealing with this often painful task is to help discern the nature of the experience of absence and to provide support and encouragement to see it through. There are no easy answers when one is alone. It does, however, make a difference in our aloneness to know that another is really not far away.

Compassion

The central message of the cross of Jesus Christ is that God has chosen to identify with the world's pain—to stand with us in our struggle so that healing might occur from within. When

millions of Jews are herded into gas chambers, when number-
less unnamed children die in Cambodia for lack of food, when
cities are destroyed by war, when a young man is murdered on
the streets of New York, when a child dies of leukemia, God
does not turn away. He weeps. That is the meaning of the
cross. It is not a rational answer to the problem of evil, nor is
it an explanation of why things do not get better. It is rather a
sign of what life is all about. The secret lies not in intellectual
accomplishment, or moral fervor, or greater achievement, all
of which can either heal or destroy, but rather in compassion,
for that alone is what heals.

Compassion is a very special word in the Christian tradition. It means "to suffer with." It takes us beyond human
cleverness, beyond moral achievement, to that place deep
within us where we can feel another human being's pain. As
Kenneth Leech states so forcefully,

> Christian spirituality is the spirituality of the Poor Man
> of Nazareth who took upon himself the form of a
> Servant. To know God is to do justice and plead the
> cause of the oppressed: to know God in Christ is to share
> in his work of establishing justice in the earth, and to
> share in his poverty and oppression.[4]

For all too many Christians the deepening of compassion is
the spiritual task most neglected, for not only is it painful, it
also raises value questions that touch the way we live and the
quality of our response to others. Elie Wiesel quotes an
ancient Hassidic rabbi as saying: "Nothing and nobody down
here frightens me, not even the angel of fear. But the moaning
of a beggar makes me shudder." Compassion, of course,
involves more than the feeling. It involves the will and the
capacity to do something to heal the pain.

As spiritual companions, we must help one another confront this most central spiritual task. To pray is to love, and to
love is to share in the life of the Compassionate One. As the

gap between the haves and the have-nots widens, and violence tears at the thin fabric of common humanity, the test of our witness will not be what we say, or even the frequency of our prayer, but the depth of our compassion.

Simplicity

The last task that I have experienced as central to our growing in Christ is the one that is probably the most difficult. How, in a world as complex as our own, can we achieve a level of simplicity that reveals the Christ in us? The answer, of course, is that we don't achieve it. It is a gift that comes as the fruit of a long and intimate relationship with the Lord. We all know people whose lives reflect this quality. Simplicity reflects an inner wisdom and a comfortableness with the wholeness of life that is bred in solitude and expressed through a certain spontaneity and joyousness that enriches every gathering in which it is found. It affects the way we live, what we need, and the way we relate to the world around us.

Although simplicity is not a quality of life that we can turn on or turn off at will, it is nevertheless a spiritual concern we can respond to. I met a person the other day who, after a few minutes' conversation, made me feel that I had known her all my life. She had a capacity to be present to me with such transparency that I felt immediately connected. As I reflect on the experience, I realize that I saw in this person a simplicity that had come from clearing away the things that often prevent people from connecting with one another—restlessness, self-absorption, hidden agendas, and the like. For those brief moments I experienced this woman for what she was, and my life was enriched. She had no need to impress me or to influence me, hence she was able to be present without deception or guile. We develop this quality first of all by wanting it, by practicing it, and by opening ourselves to what God can do when we get out of the way.

Addressing the task of more authentically reflecting the

simplicity of the Gospel, therefore, means addressing how we pray and how we live and how we relate to others. Our aim is not intensity but the joyous freedom that is found in Christ. "Take my yoke upon you, and learn from me," Jesus says, "for I am gentle and lowly in heart, and you will find rest for your souls. For my yoke is easy, and my burden is light" (Matthew 11:29-30; RSV). Herein lies the paradox of simplicity.

The Wonder of the Journey

Spiritual growth is by nature paradoxical. The more we experience inner security, the greater is our unease with the security afforded by the world. In the fourth century this sense of unease drove thousands of Christians into the desert in an effort to develop a greater sense of detachment from what they perceived to be the false security offered by the culture around them. The story of Jesus' forty days in the desert is essentially a description of his struggle to get his priorities straight. There comes a time when every Christian must seek out that desert within himself in order to find the detachment necessary to live in a new way. The attitude of the desert, writes the Chilean theologian Segundo Galilea, "is a going out of oneself to encounter the absolute and true reality of things." It allows the Christian to see what is unjust and false in the systems that shape our lives, and to give one's life to making things better. "Authentic Christian contemplation," Galilea continues, "passing through the desert, transforms contemplatives into prophets and militants into mystics."[5]

Not long ago the *New York Times* carried a story about a group of Philippine nuns who moved out of their convent to live in the streets of Manila in solidarity with the poor. As might be imagined, their move caused a great deal of comment. They were accused of being idealistic and radical. Some accused them of being Communist. Their response, however, was simple and straightforward. "We don't think of ourselves as being particularly radical," they said, "only living more boldly."

The ultimate test of our growth in Christ lies in our ability to live "more boldly" for the sake of others. There is no way we can live in this world without confronting the injustices that destroy God's creation. The momentum in our world is toward increased military build-up and toward diplomacy by threat. The risk of nuclear war has never been greater, as each year another nation achieves what is euphemistically known as "nuclear capability." At the heart of the Christian Gospel is the call for peace—peace in intent, peace in rhetoric, peace in fact. The time has come for Christians to live as becomes their faith, to speak and act "more boldly" than we have dared before.

Christian spirituality is a "spirituality for combat" that goes deep within in order to venture beyond where others dare to go. It is a life of harmony that is caught up in a rhythm between the outer and the inner, between solitude and compassion, between the desert and the city. It is open to those who in the midst of activity are able to see possibilities for ministry in response to the "still, small voice" of God. "To be a Christian and to pray are one and the same things," writes Karl Barth. "It is a matter that cannot be left to caprice. It is a need, a kind of breathing necessary to life."[6]

CHAPTER 7

The Rhythm of the Sabbath

Taste and see that the Lord is good;
happy are they who trust in him!
Psalm 34:8

Not long ago I had a very special conversation with a woman about the relationship betwen ministry and the life of prayer. This woman was a management consultant with a large firm and took her Christian commitment seriously. "To be perfectly honest," she said to me, "I don't find much support for the ministry I engage in on a day-to-day basis in the context of my work. Everything I read on prayer seems to suggest a life-style that is more suited to clergy or to people who have far more leisure time than I do."

My friend was pointing to a problem that many people experience, including most of the clergy that I know, The primary images that have shaped our understanding of the Christian spiritual tradition have come to us from the desert and the monastery. With a few notable exceptions, the pattern we have inherited presumes the possibility of regular withdrawal from an active engagement with the world in order to build a discipline that will enable us to withstand the pressure of the world. By turning inward, we are able to find the resources necessary to face outward in active engagement with the world's pain. The problem, however, lies in the fact that we often don't have time for this kind of intensive withdrawal. If we are to build a spiritual discipline we, in building it, must work from the outside in, rather than from the inside out.

What is needed, therefore, are new images of a spirituality that is more accurately described as *sanctifying time* rather than withdrawing from it. Instead of looking only to the desert or the monastery for formative images, why not also look at an even more ancient symbol from our spiritual heritage—the Sabbath? Here we have an image that emerges from the midst of our day-to-day life and seeks to redeem it. Despite its many distortions over the centuries, the Sabbath suggests a way of waiting on God that takes seriously the active lives most of us have.

The Sabbath and Christian Tradition

There has been a great deal of confusion about the place of the Sabbath in the Christian tradition. Sunday is our primary day. It is the day that commemorates the Resurrection of Christ and the beginning of new life. In the Christian tradition every Sunday, the first day of the week, is a little Easter. It replaces the seventh day as the time for celebration and worship. To speak of Sunday as the Christian Sabbath, therefore, is to confuse the issue, unless we are very careful about what we mean. "Sabbath" means something quite different from "Sunday." On the Sabbath, God rested from the six days of work in creation. He is not identical with the universe, but rather can claim lordship over it. In this sense the Sabbath expresses God's transcendence. As Charles Price and Louis Weil point out, "Human beings...are made in the image of God. When they rest from their labors, they too show that they are not identical with their work or defined by it."[1] In a world that is defined more and more by its productivity, this insight and emphasis is of particular importance, no matter how important or even sacred our work might be. It might well be that one of the central spiritual tasks for the church in our day is to rediscover the meaning of the Sabbath as a crucial part of the Christian spiritual pilgrimage, not as a day synonymous with Sunday, but as a flexible and yet distinct element of time standing beside it.

"And on the seventh day," we read in Genesis, "God finished his work which he had done, and he rested on the seventh day from all his work which he had done. So God blessed the seventh day and hallowed it, because on it God rested from all his work which he had done in creation" (2:2–3; RSV).

The origins of the Sabbath tradition lie in this passage from Genesis. How it actually developed is shrouded in mystery. The word *sabbath* most likely comes from the Hebrew word meaning "to cease" or "to stop." On the seventh day, because God rested from his labors, all creation should rest as well. As recorded in the Bible, however, the Sabbath observance is more than a participation in a special day. It is a profoundly mystical encounter with the holiness of time. As one commentator has written, "Israel not only kept the Sabbath, but contemplated it,"[2] and, strangely enough, it is the record of this contemplation, rather than of the observance, that predominates in the Old Testament.

For most Christians the idea of the Sabbath conjures up images of prohibition and joylessness, for this is indeed what we make of it. To recover the Sabbath, therefore, will require a lot of letting go. The Sabbath is fundamentally a mystical concept. Its meaning is to celebrate time rather than space. As Abraham Joshua Heschel writes, "Six days a week we live under the tyranny of the things of space; on the Sabbath we try to become attuned to the holiness of time. It is a day on which we are called upon to share in what is eternal in time, to turn from the results of creation to the mystery of creation; from the world of creation to the creation of the world."[3]

Our inner task then is to contemplate the mystery of creation. For six days God created the world of space, filling it with the hills and the sea, with trees and with streams, with animals, and ultimately with humanity itself. And then he rested for a moment in eternity, and all was still. In this stillness lies a message for us—a message that ultimately can only be grasped as the stillness within us encounters the mysterious stillness of God. "So God blessed the seventh day and hallowed it, because on it God rested from all his work which he had done in creation."

Obedience and Covenant

In the Biblical tradition, the Sabbath invites us into a relationship of obedience. It is a sign of our covenant with God. There is a story told by an ancient rabbi that illustrates this connection:

"At the beginning of the world time was one. It was eternal ... undivided and therefore translated to the world of space. In order that time be related to space, God in His wisdom divided it into seven days so that an intimate relationship between time and space might forever be established. With every single day, another realm of things came into being, except on the seventh day. The Sabbath, we are told, was a lonely day.

"After the work of creation was completed, the seventh day pleaded, 'Master of Universe, all that thou hast created is in couples: to every day in the week thou gavest a mate, only I was left alone.' And God answered, 'The community of Israel will be your mate'....That promise was not forgotten. When the people of Israel stood before the mountain of Sinai, the Lord said to them, 'Remember that I said to the Sabbath, *the Community of Israel is your mate.* Hence, remember the Sabbath day to sanctify it.'"[4]

At the heart of this ancient story lies a fundamental truth: Our relationship to time can never be one of convenience. It is a covenant that stands at the heart of creation itself. We have been called into a covenant with time for our very life's sake. Our relationship to the Sabbath, therefore, however we express it, is a relationship not of convenient choice, but of covenant obedience. "Remember the sabbath day, to keep it holy," comes the commandment. "Six days you shall labor, and do all your work; but the seventh day is a sabbath to the Lord your God" (Exodus 20:8–10; RSV). And from the prophet Jeremiah came even stronger words: "Take heed for the sake of your lives, and do not bear a burden on the sabbath day or bring it in by the gates of Jerusalem. And do not carry a burden out of your houses on the sabbath or do any work, but keep the sabbath day holy, as I commanded your fathers. Yet they did not listen or incline their ear, but stiffened their neck, that they might not hear and receive instruction" (17:21–23; RSV).

As a Biblical people, we are bound together with the Sabbath in a covenant of obedience. The commandment to hallow the Sabbath is not, therefore, peripheral to our relationship with God. It is an invitation to enter into covenant with reality. For when the Sabbath is ignored, the world will ultimately consume itself by the force of its own energy and greed.

To obey the Sabbath precept means that we seek to set aside a "day" in each week in which we will quite consciously contemplate the world rather than contest it. In each of us the "day" might vary in length according to circumstances. It will be prepared for by contemplative time set aside on other days, and it will seek to relate us to Sunday in a new way. But the point is, the call to hallow time in the midst of our busyness is ultimately a question not of convenience but of obedience. To understand what is being asked of us in terms less than this is to miss the seriousness of what is implied. The idea of the Sabbath rest is concerned with nothing less than the survival of creation itself.

Obedience to God is not a concept that we speak of much in the church today, and yet it is a concept that is central to the spiritual life (as I have written elsewhere). "For most of us the word immediately conjures up thoughts of passivity, blind submission or the rules and regulations placed upon us in childhood. In theological terms, however, obedience is a covenant word. We are partners in a covenant of love initiated by God. Jesus lived his life in obedience to this covenant. Our obedience is our response to what He has done.... 'Obedience,' writes Jacques Ellul, 'is an active struggle with all that impedes the reality of the life in Christ.' It is out of our sense of obedience that we discover the motivation necessary for a disciplined life."[5]

As Christians we are called to live in the world in a different way—not in some pseudo-pious way that is totally out of touch with reality, but in a way that offers some options to a world consumed by the frenzy of its own activity. For this is what the obedience of vocation means, and there comes a time when each of us must face the consequences, both to ourselves and to the world, of letting our obedience dim.

The Inner Sabbath

"The Sabbath was made for the sake of man and not man for the Sabbath," Jesus proclaimed to the Pharisees. "Therefore," he said, "the Son of Man is sovereign even over the Sabbath" (Mark 2:27–28; NEB). With these words Jesus challenged the ancient Halakah tradition of Sabbath observance and reaffirmed the Sabbath as an inner state that reflects our attitude toward the world around us and toward the relationship of intimacy offered us by God.

Jesus' radical pronouncement regarding the Sabbath observance comes in the context of two stories recorded by the Synoptic writers with relatively little difference between each of the Gospel versions. In the first story, as Mark tells it, Jesus was walking with his disciples on the Sabbath when they began to pluck ears of grain. The Pharisees were deeply offended at what was an obvious transgression of the Sabbath law. Jesus defended his disciples' action by referring to the time that David and his men had eaten the sacred altar bread (an action analogous, if you will, to eating the reserved sacrament) because they were hungry and had nothing else to eat.

The point Jesus seems to be making is that our relation to the Sabbath is essentially an inner state. The Sabbath is an expression of time which provides a context in which we might view the world from the vantage point of an intimate experience of God. Because the disciples were sharing in that intimacy as they walked through the cornfield with Jesus, they were free to view the Sabbath from the perspective of need rather than law.

The second story involves the action of Jesus alone. Quite intentionally, the Pharisees brought Jesus a man with a withered arm to see whether or not he would heal him on the Sabbath. According to the law, to break the Sabbath deliberately was a capital offense. Capital punishment, however, could only be inflicted if the convicted perpetrator had demonstrably been warned before witnesses and if it was made certain that he had acted deliberately. The first of these two Sabbath stories reports the giving of the warning to Jesus and his explanation that he was treating the Sabbath as a matter of conviction. The second story makes the judgment final. Despite the previous warning, he healed the man with the withered hand because not to do so would be contrary to the law of love. The new age had come, and the law of life was the love manifested by God in Christ. It was the acting out of this conviction that brought Jesus to the cross, and on the cross he sets us free.

These two stories have profound implications for the Christian spiritual pilgrimage. They exalt flexibility over rigid conformity to rule. They call us to adapt our spiritual lives to the circumstances that confront us, realizing that the circumstances are continually changing. A spiritual discipline that works today, therefore, might not be helpful tomorrow. But more than this, Christ's sovereignty over the Sabbath calls us to view the Sabbath not necessarily as a set day of the week, but as a state of being that we embrace intentionally at an invitation from God.

In a chapter entitled "Meditation and Sabbath" in his book *Turning East,* Harvey Cox suggests that the spirit of the Sabbath "is a biblical equivalent of meditation. It nurtures the same kind of awareness that meditation nurtures, for Sabbath is not just a day for doing nothing. It is a particular form of consciousness, a way of thinking and being that strongly resembles what the Buddhists call 'mindfulness.'"[6] In the Hassidic tradition of Judaism, Cox points out, the Sabbath not only excludes our ordinary form of intervening and ordering, it also excludes manipulative ways of thinking about the world. He illustrates this by quoting a story told by Abraham Joshua Heschel:

> A certain rabbi, it seems, who was renowned for his wisdom and piety, and especially for his zeal in keeping Sabbath, once took a leisurely walk in the garden on the Sabbath day—an activity which even the severest interpreters allowed. Strolling in the shade of the branches the rabbi noticed that one of the apple trees badly needed pruning. Recognizing that, of course, such a thing could not be done on the seventh day, the rabbi nonetheless made a mental note to himself that he would see to the pruning early the next week.... But when the rabbi went out to the tree a few days later with ladder and clippers, he found it shriveled and lifeless. God had destroyed the apple tree to teach the rabbi that even *thinking* about work on the Sabbath is a violation of the commandment and of the true spirit of the Holy Day.[7]

"It is a matter of consciousness," Cox points out. "When we plan to prune a tree, we perceive it differently than we do when we are simply aware of it, allowing it—for the moment at least—simply to be as it is."[8] This, I believe, is a fundamental principle of Christian spirituality. What must we do in the ordering of our time to be able to see again? We are blinded by the busyness and the distortion that dominate our culture. The issue is not so much our need to pray as it is our need to see. For when we begin to see the world as it is in the eyes of Christ, prayer becomes a natural mode of existence.

"The Sabbath was made for the sake of man and not man for the Sabbath," Jesus reminds us. He is sovereign, and incites us to reshape an ancient tradition not only for our own soul or health but for the sake of the world. What we see, and the way we see, is a matter of consciousness. In Christ we are given the eyes of faith. The blind man was brought to Jesus, asking to see. Jesus spat on his eyes and asked if he could see anything. "I see men as trees walking," he said. He was still holding back, not ready to trust fully. So Jesus laid hands on his eyes, and in a triumph of healing faith, the former blind man could see clearly. This, as we all know in our heart of hearts, is precisely what is offered to us.

The Outer Sabbath

Sabbath spirituality ultimately connects us with the suffering of God, for it calls us to account for the suffering of humanity. "Six days you shall do your work," we read in the Book of Exodus, "but on the seventh day you shall rest; that your ox and your ass may have rest, and the son of your bondmaid, and the alien, may be refreshed" (23:12; RSV).

The Sabbath rest is not solely a matter of personal piety. We rest in solidarity with those whose burden is heavy. In this basic insight there is contained a long and deep concern for human liberation. The ancient Hebrews were enjoined to plant their fields for six years, and on the seventh year to let them lie fallow. The crops that grew on these resting fields were made available to the poor. From such simple beginnings, too, emerged the idea of the Jubilee. After seven seven-year periods (that is, in the fiftieth year) a jubilee was declared, in which debts were forgiven and prisoners released—a theme echoed in Jesus' own statement of ministry. Sabbath spirituality is a spirituality of compassion, for it links us directly with the plight of the oppressed.

One of the great theological tasks of our age is to reunite spirituality with compassion. Prayer means nothing if it does not ultimately connect us with the pain of others and motivate us to seek to heal that pain.

Henri Nouwen tells a story that suggests what such spirituality might mean to those of us who have chosen to live by the sign of the cross.

> Once there was a very old man who used to meditate early every morning under a large tree on the bank of the Ganges River in India. One morning, having finished his meditation, the old man opened his eyes and saw a scorpion floating helplessly in the strong current of the river. As the scorpion was pulled closer to the tree, it got caught in the long tree roots. The scorpion struggled frantically to free itself but got more and more entangled in the complex network of the tree roots.
>
> When the old man saw this, he immediately stretched himself onto the extended roots and reached out to rescue the drowning scorpion. But as soon as he touched it, the animal jerked and stung him wildly. Instinctively, the man withdrew his hand, but then, after having regained his balance, he once again stretched himself out along the roots to save the scorpion. Every time the old man came within reach, the scorpion stung him so badly with its poisonous tail that his hand became swollen and bloody and his face distorted with pain.
>
> At that moment, a passer-by saw the old man stretched out on the roots struggling with the scorpion and shouted, "Hey, stupid old man. What's wrong with you? Only a fool risks his life for such an ugly useless creature. Don't you know you may kill yourself trying to save that ungrateful animal?" Slowly the old man turned his head, and looking calmly in the stranger's eyes, he

said, "Friend, because it is of the nature of the scorpion
to sting, why should I give up my nature to save?"⁹

This, of course, is the spiritual problem that faces us all.
Just because the world bites, just because our efforts so often
go unappreciated, just because the problem of human suffering seems almost overwhelming, just because there is so little
time—why should we give up our nature to be compassionate
in both what we feel and the way we live?

Speaking personally, there is no other problem in the
spiritual life that I find more difficult that coming to terms
with all it means to be a compassionate person. The degree of
pain that confronts me on the streets of New York alone, not
to mention the daily barrage I receive from the media, has a
way of deadening my sensitivity to *all* pain—at least deadening it to such a degree that my desire to act in response to what
I feel is so minimal as to be almost totally ineffective. I think
this is a particular problem for those of us who are confronted
with personal suffering every day. It is hard to move beyond
our own immediate world.

If we are to bear witness to the solidarity of creation,
somewhere in our lives there must be room for a more global
compassion. For this kind of compassion can change the way
we live. We will consume less when we are aware of the pain of
those who have nothing to eat. We will work for disarmament
and world peace when deep within us we are confronted by
the indescribable suffering of war. To feel at this level is to
participate in the pain of God.

Sabbath spirituality is not solely a matter of a personal
piety. We rest, let go, desist, stand back, to experience both
the awesomeness of creation and the awfulness of human
pain. To know these is to know what it means to live in
Christ—to live *in* and *with* the One who embraced the agony
of human suffering that he might move through and beyond
it, transforming the worst into a sign of new life. In him is our

hope for the world. Indeed, it is the ministry that we are called
to share.

A Sabbath Style of Life

"Look carefully then how you walk, not as unwise men [and
women] but as wise, making the most of the time [or, as the
King James Version reads, "redeeming the time"] because the
days are evil" (Ephesians 5:15–16; RSV).

We redeem the time when we allow a moment or a series of
moments to become for us a vehicle of God's presence. To
redeem the time is to make time transparent so that we
experience it not as pressure ("Hurry up, hurry up, we haven't
enough time"), but as a sign of the holy. Obviously, we can't
always live this way, but we can live in such a way that the
redemption of time becomes an ongoing and consistent
possibility. I call this living in a Sabbath rhythm, and I am
more and more convinced that the development of such a
rhythm is at the heart of the recovery of authentic spirituality.

We can begin living in a Sabbath rhythm by deliberately
setting aside one day in the week that will be lived differently
from the rest. For some people Sunday becomes this kind of
day. It seems to me, however, that this tends to confuse the
issue. For the Christian, the Sabbath is not the same as
Sunday; it is a preparation for Sunday. The idea is to take one
day a week and deliberately slow it down. Our sabbath can be
Saturday or a regular workday, but it is a day that is planned.

We begin the day with a prayer of simple awareness, which
of course can take many forms. One way is to let your mind,
at the point of awakening, focus on all that surrounds you,
without analyzing or judging. Simply take note of what you
see and hear—the room, the light, the sounds. Be aware of
yourself and of the life that has been given you and, at this
moment of awareness, place the day in God's keeping.

I know of one person who on his Sabbath day deliberately
slows down his motions in order to sharpen his awareness. He

brushes his teeth more slowly, walks more slowly, until the day's rhythm is established. I was just recently told of a lawyer in New York who makes it a point to spend five minutes in silent contemplation between clients, in order to be fully present to the person when he or she comes in. He calls this part of his Sabbath rhythm—a way of acknowledging the holiness of time.

Sabbath observance can take many forms. It might involve an intentional fast in solidarity with the deprivation of the hungry peoples of the world, or a special meal cooked with care and offered in some special way.

A couple I know made a visit to an art gallery an experience of Sabbath observance. Together they tried to see what was before them more deeply, and were thus helped to see one another more deeply. I have a friend who observes his Sabbath by deliberately and intentionally seeking to silently identify with the strangers on the street, from the most elegant to the most wretched.

All these are ways of living more intentionally in the spirit of the Sabbath. If we must work, we work in ways that allow the moments to be hallowed. Barbara Crassner, a Jewish woman writing in *Liturgy* magazine, put it in this way: "For me, as for my forebears, the Sabbath as an event remains a path to healing. It is a way of facing separation and meeting, death and rebirth, and other significant processes of life through the tools of real relating, presence, listening, imagination, response and reparation. For me, as for my forebears," she continues, "the Sabbath embodies a concern for inner unity and inter-human equity through the tools of personal piety, study, song and prayer."

Human solidarity will never be achieved in this world unless there are structures built into our lives that allow for a deliberate change in consciousness. Solidarity is a spiritual experience. Without it there can be no lasting compassion or concern for the totality of life on the planet earth. The rhythm of the Sabbath, regardless of how it is expressed, is a way of taking the world back to its roots.

It is obvious that in the kind of pluralism in which we live today there is no way that the Sabbath in its old form can be established as a universal observance. As Harvey Cox rightly points out, "The greed of an acquisitive society, the pace of industrial production—signaled by lights that never go out and belts that move day and night, all week and all year—the historic Christian contempt for the Jewish religious vision, the compulsive rationalism of a truncated form of science, all these have conspired to create a mindset in the modern West"[10] which mitigates against the very things we might need most. "What we need," Cox says, "is a form of Sabbath observance which can be practiced in the modern, pluralistic world, which can function on an individual or a small group basis, but which restores the lost dialectic of action and repose, of intervention and letting be."[11]

In six days God created the earth, and on the seventh day he rested. And "God blessed the seventh day and hallowed it, because on it God rested from all his work which he had done in creation."

To live by a Sabbath rhythm is to bear witness—witness to those intangible things that are so necessary for our survival. And those things—the integrity of family life, friendships, caring for one another, seeing and hearing in new ways, living in the presence of God—are supported and helped to happen by a life lived with a Sabbath rhythm.

Living in Expectation

Christian ministry is born in solitude, expressed through an active caring for the world and the people in it, and sustained by an openness to the presence of God in every aspect of human life. It is a way of life that allows us to find solitude even when we are surrounded by people: solitude involves being alone with God. There are times when this will mean withdrawal and a significant change of pace. There are other times when solitude is found in walking on a city street, in quietly praying for a stranger, or in simply being still in the midst of activity. Underlying all this is a sense of expectation—the sense that in the most mundane experience, there is always the possibility of meeting God in a new way.

It is my conviction that the re-establishment of the Sabbath rhythm is not only necessary for living the Christian life more fully, but also necessary for enabling the world to get in touch with its root values. But for the Christian the rhythm of the Sabbath can never be an end in itself. It points beyond itself to that moment in which God entered history in the person of Jesus Christ and gave us a new understanding of time. The days of the week, numbered one to seven, recall the story of creation in the first chapter of Genesis. On the eighth day, however, the day when the cycle begins again, we celebrate the gift of new life offered to us in the Resurrection. The eighth day becomes for the Christian the symbol of the completion of creation in the Kingdom of God. In Christ the sanctification of time is made complete. For the Christian, therefore, the rhythm of the Sabbath leads us to the eighth day. The Christian life is one of expectation embodied in the celebration of the Eucharist. Here, all people, all meditation, all compassion, all human relationships are caught up and made new in that sacramental action where past and future are made one.

"Creation is the language of God," writes Abraham Joshua Heschel, "time is his song, and things of space the consonants in the song. To sanctify time is to sing the vowels in unison with him. This is the task of humanity—to conquer space and sanctify time."[12]

When this happens, ministry and solitude are no longer separate but one simple expression of the life of Christ.

Epilogue

*Let everything that has breath
praise the Lord. Hallelujah!*
Psalm 150:6

In Walker Percy's novel *The Second Coming,* Will Barrett concludes a humorous but rather biting description of the vast range of beliefs characteristic of the American religious scene with this almost haunting question: "Is this image of belief," he asks, "a great renaissance of faith after a period of mass materialism, atheism, agnosticism, liberalism, scientism? Or is it an age of madness in which everyone believes everything? Which?"[1]

In responding to Will Barrett's question I find myself caught on the horns of a dilemma. I happen to believe that we are experiencing, throughout the world, a new age of faith, but I also believe that, because of the very close link that exists between so much of what might be called a renewal of faith and the insecurity of our times, we are also experiencing much of what Will Barrett refers to as "madness," madness being defined here as fervor without critique. I believe very strongly that the time has come for a case to be made once again for an expression of Christianity that treats the intellectual and humanistic gains of civilization with respect rather than alarm. I acknowledge with appreciation much that I have experienced and learned from the renewal movements that are sweeping the church. I admit that the new association of fundamentalist religion with the political right has arisen in part as a legitimate protest against an apparent confusion of values and against the failure of those in power to hear the voices of a segment of our culture. I am concerned, however, about the shape and content of a faith that is cut off from the historic concerns of what is often referred to as "liberal" Christianity—concerns for such things as intellectual rigor, social justice, and the gap that exists between the sacred and secular. The recent and reoccurring attempts to pit the biblical story of creation against scientific theories about the origins of life is, for many thoughtful people, an attempt to compare apples and oranges, an attempt that leads ultimately not to greater faith, but to greater confusion. Conviction alone is not enough. We are called to engage the world with the wisdom of serpents and the gentleness of doves.

Christian ministry is a ministry of the whole person. It is an expression of the life of Christ, a life that at every point must confront the world as it is—not only critically, but with the awareness that it is in the world, with all of its complexity, that God chooses to reveal himself. In solitude we await God. We await him as he reveals himself in the deep silence of our lives and in the dreams and ongoing reflections that constitute our life experience. We await him as he reveals himself in the presence of another human being, for this, too, is an experience of solitude. Ministry, as has been said before, is not born in activity, but in solitude. It is the natural expression of our ongoing life with the risen Lord. Christian ministry has meaning to the degree that it reflects both the spirit and the substance of Christ's ministry to the world. It is in him alone that we live out our baptism, but we do so not separated from the world but in dialogue with it.

We make a mistake when we identify ministry with being "religious." Compared with many of the adherents of the established religions of this day, Jesus was not a "religious" person. He was less concerned with the outward expression of religion and more concerned with what went on within. He ate with tax collectors and sinners. He laughed and he cried. He affirmed the goodness of life even in the midst of its pain. The invitation of his life is not to be more religious, but more holy, and there is a decided difference. Being religious, in the commonly accepted sense of the word, calls attention to one's self; holiness reflects the holiness of God.

I believe that the task of the church today is to engage the world at every level with the claims and values of the Gospel. For this to happen we need a ministry of clergy and laity who understand who they are and to whom they belong, who are committed to reflecting this identity in every aspect of their lives. At the heart of this understanding of ministry is what I would call a holy worldliness—a commitment to participate in the struggle of the world as one who knows the Lord. Holy worldliness is life-affirming rather than pleasure-denying. It calls people to faith, not out of guilt or fear, but out of a vision of God that *evokes* response rather than commands it. It is a way of living shaped by the words, "And God created the world and it was good." It does not deny the awful reality of human sin, but rather emphasizes what redemption in Christ makes possible. It affirms wholeness and sexuality and human pleasure, not as ends in themselves, but as reflections of the love of God.

We are surrounded by forces that seek to motivate us by playing on our guilt and our fear and our understandable frustration and concern over so much that goes on. There are days when it feels as if only simple answers and clearly defined enemies will satisfy the uneasiness we feel. To give in to these feelings, however, is to deny something that is fundamental to our baptism. We are a people of promise who, even in the midst of death, can proclaim hope. We have been given a vision of the world that sees the presence of God in the simple and in the complex, in the discoveries of science and in the pain and drama of the city. The call to ministry is a call, not to back away from these things, but to see in all that the world presents the mystery of both the presence and the absence of God. When our relationship to Jesus Christ is nurtured in community and solitude and draws on all the senses and all the gifts God has given us as human beings, then we need not fear the hard questions that the world proposes. We need not fear uncertainty or new ideas or even doubt, for Jesus Christ is our hope and our promise, yesterday, today, and tomorrow. The Christian pilgrimage is not easy or without pain, but it gives to countless millions meaning and new possibilities in their lives.

> "Behold! I am making all things new!" writes the author of the Book of Revelation. "A draught from the water-springs of life will be my free gift to the thirsty" (21:5,6; NEB).

NOTES

Chapter 1

1. *Action Information,* June 1980. (The Alban Institute, Mt. St. Alban, Washington, D.C. 20016).

2. Elizabeth O'Connor, *Eighth Day of Creation: Gifts and Creativity* (Waco, Texas: Word, Inc., 1971), p. 23.

3. Henri Nouwen, *With Open Hands* (Notre Dame, Indiana: Ave Maria Press, 1972), p. 12.

4. Kenneth Leech, *Soul Friend* (New York: Harper & Row, 1974), pp. 130-131.

5. Kenneth Leech, *True Prayer* (London: Sheldon Press, 1980), p. 79.

Chapter 2

1. For a fuller development of this theme see the Joe Morris Doss article "The Unified Symbol of Ministry: Sacramental Orders," in the *Anglican Theological Review* (January 1980), Vol. LXII, No. 1, p. 20.

2. Urban T. Holmes, *Ministry and Imagination* (New York: The Seabury Press, 1976). See especially Chapter V, pp. 111-136.

3. Quoted by Martin Marty in *Context* (Chicago: Clarendon Publications, 1981).

Chapter 3

1. For more detailed discussion of these categories see David McLelland's *The Achieving Society* (New York: Halstead Press, 1976) and *The Inner Experience* (New York: Irvington Publishers, Inc., 1979).

2. Johannes B. Metz, *Poverty of Spirit* (New York: Paulist Press, 1968), p. 25.

3. Henri Nouwen, *The Wounded Healer* (Garden City, N.Y.: Doubleday/Image, 1972), pp. 99–100.

Chapter 4

1. Bernard Cooke, *Ministry to Word and Sacrament* (Philadelphia: Fortress Press, 1976), p. 203.

2. James D. Anderson and Ezra Earl Jones, *The Management of Ministry* (New York: Harper & Row, 1978), pp. 196–197.

3. Jean Haldane, *Religious Pilgrimage* (The Alban Institute, Mt. St. Alban, Washington, D.C. 20016).

4. May Sarton, *Journal of a Solitude* (New York: W.W. Norton and Co., 1973), pp. 98–99.

5. Parker Palmer, *Going Public* (The Alban Institute, Mt. St. Alban, Washington, D.C. 20016), p. 6.

Chapter 5

1. Norman Pittenger, *Unbounded Love* (New York: The Seabury Press, 1976), p. 27.

2. John Futrell, S.J., "Communal Discernment: Reflections on Experience," *Studies in the Spirituality of the Jesuits* (November 1972), Vol. IV, No. 5, p. 173.

3. ibid., p. 173.

4. William Stringfellow, *An Ethic for Christians and Other Aliens in a Strange Land* (Waco, Texas: Word, Inc., 1979), p. 78.

5. Quoted in Michael Mildenberger, "Spirituality as Alternative," *Ecumenical Review* (July 1979), Vol. 29, No. 3, p. 299.

Chapter 6

1. T.S. Eliot, *Four Quartets,* in *The Complete Poems and Plays* of T.S. Eliot (New York: Harcourt, Brace and Co., 1953), p. 145.

2. Kosuki Koyama, *No Handle on the Cross* (Maryknoll, N.Y.: Orbis Books, 1977), p. 30.

3. Ignatius Loyola, *Spiritual Exercises* (Garden City, N.Y.: Doubleday/Image), p. 131.

4. Kenneth Leech, *True Prayer* (London: Sheldon Press, 1980), p. 73.

5. Segundo Galilea, "Politics and Contemplation," *The Mystical and Political Dimensions of the Christian Faith,* Geffre and Gutierrez, eds. (New York: Herder and Herder, 1974), p. 28.

6. Karl Barth, *Prayer* (Philadelphia: Westminster, 1952), p. 231.

Chapter 7

1. Charles Price and Louis Weil, *Liturgy for Living* (New York: The Seabury Press, 1980), p. 225.

2. Niels-Erick Anderson, *The Old Testament Sabbath* (Society of Biblical Literature, Dissertation Series #7, 1972), p. 14.

3. Abraham Joshua Heschel, *The Sabbath: Its Meaning for Modern Man* (New York: Farrar, Straus and Young, Inc., 1951), p. 10.

4. Ibid., pp. 51–52.

5. James C. Fenhagen, *More Than Wanderers* (New York: The Seabury Press, 1978), p. 59.

6. Harvey Cox, *Turning East* (New York: Simon and Schuster, 1977), p. 69.

7. ibid., p. 70.

8. ibid., p. 70.

9. This is a story that Henri Nouwen, the great priest-teacher-writer, has told in many of his lectures.

10. Cox, op. cit., p. 72.

11. ibid., p. 71.

12. Heschel, op. cit., p. 101.

Epilogue

1. Walker Percy, *The Second Coming* (New York: Farrar, Straus & Giroux, 1980), p. 159.

jn it well 10